17.63
3000.
1

1000
2.+1.8
BRUCE.

BOSNIA JOURNAL

**An American Civilian's Account of His Service
With the 1st Armored Division
And the Russian Brigade
In Bosnia**

December 1995-November 1996

By James Nelson

INFINITY PUBLISHING

ISBN 0-7414-2321-9

Author's Web site
www.geocities.com/hillcountryrussian

Published by:

INFINITY
PUBLISHING.COM

1094 New De Haven Street, Suite 100
West Conshohocken, PA 19428-2713
Info@buybooksontheweb.com
www.buybooksontheweb.com
Toll-free (877) BUY BOOK
Local Phone (610) 941-9999
Fax (610) 941-9959

Printed in the United States of America

Printed on Recycled Paper

Published March 2005

Dedicated to

Rosemary, Emily, Nika,
And
All Those Who Serve Good Causes

Table of Contents

Preface

My journal as typed out on these pages is substantially the same as it was when it was originally written out by hand at the times and places indicated. A few omissions have been made and occasional corrections of style and fact have been made. Additions made are either dated or they were made after my return from Bosnia. In both instances such materials are enclosed by square brackets: [....]. Phonetic transcriptions of place and personal names are also enclosed by square brackets.

I was a Department of the Army employee at the George C. Marshall Center for European Security Studies at Garmisch-Partenkirchen, Germany, but I bear sole responsibility for the presentation of facts and opinions in this journal. My presentation of them may or may not coincide with the official positions of the United States Government on them.

Tuzla Air Base (TAB)
Bosnia and Herzegovina
Tues 19 Dec 1995
1015-1600 hrs

This morning it is snowing lightly in Tuzla. The temperature must be about 30F (about -1C).

We arrived by C-130 at 2230 hrs yesterday in a drizzling rain. "We" were two Humvees (the current Army replacement for the Jeep) and Major General William L. Nash and entourage—about 40 people. GEN Nash is CG (Commanding General) of 1 AD (1st Armored Division, United States Army). The 1 AD is to attempt to enforce the peace in the American sector of Bosnia and Herzegovina for a period of about a year following the signing of the Peace Agreement in Paris on 14 Dec.

I am Jim Nelson, civilian interpreter for GEN Nash in all his dealings with COL Aleksandr Ivanovich Lentsov, commander of the Russian brigade, which falls under the operational control of GEN Nash. I wear BDUs (battle dress uniform), so I look more or less like any American soldier, except that I wear no insignia of any kind. So far my duties have consisted primarily of watching baggage (last night—it was about 0200 hrs this morning before I was assigned and occupied a place to sleep) and watching people's rifles when they leave the room here at HQ (Headquarters). In about three weeks, when the permanent Russian contingent arrives, I will move to their HQ. I asked for this job.

In my other life I am James Nelson, [age 57,] PhD, GS-12, Chairman of the Russian Dept at FLTCE (the Foreign Language Training Center Europe) at the George C. Marshall Center for European Security Studies in Garmisch-Partenkirchen, Germany, in the Bavarian Alps right next to the Austrian border.

A Russian recon group consisting of a couple of generals and COL Lentsov is expected here sometime today.

1

The way I got involved is that I was asked to interpret for GEN Nash and COL Lentsov at their initial meetings at permanent 1 AD HQ in Bad Kreuznach, Germany, 26-30 November. It was then that I hit up GEN Nash for this job. My immediate supervisor at 1 AD is Major John Bushyhead. He speaks Russian, too, but not as well as I do.

Actually, I spent (and will spend) most of my time with staff personnel, Russian and American, and COL Lentsov, and comparatively little with GEN Nash.

Practically everyone, Russian and American, calls me "Jim"; I do not call the General "Bill." GEN Nash treats people in a folksy, friendly sort of way, but I have not noticed anyone being folksy with him. GEN Nash is of medium height with dark hair. He wears glasses. He is from Arizona. His father [if I have it correctly] was commander of the last horse-mounted cavalry brigade in the United States Army. That was in 1940. GEN Nash served in Vietnam and in Desert Storm (1990-91) he commanded the 1st Brigade of the 3rd Armored Division. [Major Tom Haines says the 1st BDE was the largest maneuver BDE in Germany when it was sent off to the Persian Gulf. Personal communication, Dec 1996; entered 6 Apr 97; corrected 7 Sep 04.]

COL Lentsov will be 39 tomorrow (20 Dec 95). He has been a full colonel of Russian airborne troops since he was 33 and is a protégé of GEN (retired) Aleksandr Lebed, probable candidate for President of Russia in June 1996.

At about 1230 we rushed out to the airstrip in a white (beneath the mud) UN van to meet the Russians, who had supposedly landed. We chased around for about 20 minutes looking for them, but never did find them. Eventually we learned that this was because there weren't any Russians, not yet, at least.

I must have been unconscious when I came in to HQ this morning, because when, during our chasing around, Major Bushyhead posted me in front of HQ in case a Russian general wandered in alone, I mistakenly walked into the UN HQ building across the Big Muddy (our street), and when I couldn't find us on either floor, I finally asked where the hell

GEN Nash was. Turned out that GEN Nash is on the first and only floor of the building across from the UN.

Nothing at 1 AD HQ, or indeed anything at Tuzla Air Base, is elegant.

An Air Force guy (or some other kind of guy, I'm not sure) was just here seeking help unloading shitters [sic]. Major Bushyhead said he'd be glad to help, but generally the Army prefers trees. And anyway, Major Lorenz is in charge of shitters, which, incidentally, come in quite a variety of models, but that's not my specialty, either, and so I don't remember what they were.

COL Lentsov is a paratrooper who has jumped out of airplanes 565 times. He fought in Afghanistan, and on New Year's Eve and New Year's Day last year (1994-5) participated in the disastrous Russian assault on Grozny, Chechnya. He says it was the worst experience of his life, and I think it may have profoundly affected his attitude toward the whole business of war. How to describe Lentsov: larger-than-life, over six feet tall, broad-shouldered, narrow-waisted, blue eyes, light brown hair, regular features granite-hewn, good speaking voice (although it doesn't match Lebed's bass). Lentsov is from a working-class family in Krasnodar, in the Kuban region of southern Russia, to the northeast of the Black Sea, not very far, in fact, from Chechnya. He is of Kuban Cossack origin, but he has nothing but contempt for those who prance around now in bemedalled Cossack uniforms just because their grandfathers or great-grandfathers really were Cossacks. He speaks with a noticeable southern Russian accent. (It is much less pronounced than that of his compatriot from the Russian south, Mikhail Sergeyevich Gorbachev, whom he reviles as the greatest traitor of our time for causing the collapse of the Soviet Union. The reason for the difference in accents is probably that Lentsov grew up in an urban center, while Gorbachev is a country boy.) On the one hand Lentsov saw nothing fundamentally wrong with the Soviet system, and on the other, he has a passionate hatred for purveyors of ideology, among whom he includes also those who peddle or

3

pretend to revere religion from high places [as it were]. He says it is the working stiff, and also the elderly, who have taken it in the neck in recent years, and he's right about that. He says Russia is plenty big enough as it is, and anyway, Russia never has and does not now seek to incorporate other people's lands by force, but at the same time it is totally ridiculous that Ukraine should be a country separate and distinct from Russia. There is no such thing as a bad people—there are only bad individuals—but there is something wrong with the Estonians, he says. The best form of government for Russia would be a democratic authoritarianism, elections being a pointless exercise. He does perceive that America is a state founded in law and Russia's great misfortune is that it is not. I remarked that his and my life experiences are very different and that we would just have to agree to disagree about some things. He said sure, fine, that was the civilized thing to do.

Lentsov is not in possession of very much social couth, and he positively revels in being a Russian bear, including the hug. He sometimes uses extreme, obscenity-laced language in dressing down subordinates. One of the subordinates, seeing how appalled I apparently looked, said that there was no need to worry, that Lentsov would cool down soon enough. But Lentsov was shocked when similar language was used at a US Army briefing at which some of the people present were women. I responded that they weren't there as women, but as officers in our Army, which no one, after all, had compelled them to join. He replied that just the same it wasn't right.

Here is a joke COL Lentsov related on 10 Dec 95 in Bad Kreuznach. A note: Chukchis are a people related to Eskimos and the popular perception of them in Russia is that they are dumb and so they are the butt of a lot of jokes. This is probably a very un-PC joke.

The Chukcha was the best hunter in the village. He'd see a squirrel and BANG, he'd get it right in the eye. Another squirrel, BANG, and he'd get it right in the eye. In this way the Chukcha would bring in about 50 squirrels a day.

One day when the Chukcha was out shooting squirrels suddenly two jet fighter planes appeared and began doing all kinds of aerobatics: barrel rolls, coming together, flying apart, etc. The Chukcha was so fascinated by the spectacle that he ended up with his right eye looking far to the right at the same time that his left eye looked far to the left. That day he only brought in three squirrels.

The people in the village were concerned about their Chukcha now that he couldn't see very well with his two eyes looking off in different directions and they called for the doctor to come from town and see if he couldn't help the Chukcha.

The doctor came, examined the Chukcha, and told him what to do to recover his vision. "What you should do," the doctor said, "is to put a nut on your nose and concentrate looking at the nut for two or three weeks and in that way you should recover your vision."

When the doctor came back to the village three weeks later to see how his patient was doing, the people in the village told him that the Chukcha had died.

"How did that happen?" the doctor asked.

"Well, the Chukcha was able to get a nut up to his chin, but it wouldn't stretch any further and he died."

1715 hrs
Major Lorenz (on the telephone): "This place is just in chaos... We're never gonna house all these people."

1820
"Four-star place. French cuisine, Pate de..." The reference is to the French equivalent of our MREs (Meals, Ready to Eat) that seem to be in relative abundance in the building.

The Russians are supposedly coming in by road from Brcko [BRCH-ko]. Why that way I don't know. I'm praying they will get here so late they'll be put up for the night and I can go on the platform more or less rested. Otherwise I'll be running mainly on adrenaline.

Major Lorenz: "Unbelievable.... I've had a lot of fun today."

GEN Cherrie an hour or so ago: "Clean this God-damned place up. And shut up when people are on the phone!"

Later he came in and was entirely cordial with me and said I only had to ask if there was anything they could do for me.

GEN Cherrie lost two fingers on his right hand in Vietnam. He seems to limp a little, too. [He stepped on a mine in Vietnam and besides the fingers lost his right leg below the knee.]

Wed, 20 Dec 95 0820

The Russians, 14 of them, none familiar to me, finally arrived at about 1930. They had flown three hours from Moscow to Belgrade, and then drove all day, coming in from the north through Brcko and the Posavina Corridor. After GEN Cherrie's briefing and about an hour of waiting for accommodations for them, the Major and I left them at about 2215. They were impressed that we put some people out on the floor in the corridor of the "hotel" so that they could have bunk beds. And in general they said that they were impressed by how well we received them.

0826
I'm off to meet them now. Today I'll earn my pay.

1930
I got back to the container I share with COL Stratman at about 1900 and would have been here half an hour sooner if I had been able to find my way here from HQ, which is right next door, without getting very persistently lost. This morning I was able to follow instructions and find the Russians, who are at some distance, but I couldn't go the other way, although this morning I walked right past the HQ

on the way to the Russians. It's Major Lorenz's fault: he gave me a ride home last night instead of saying, "Walk that way about 100 feet and you're on the left." But why we drove five minutes to get here I can't imagine.

It was foggy all day and only one plane landed.

Thanks to the Russians, some of whom are from the UN contingent, I got slipped into the UN dining hall and had a hot dinner and supper today. But unless I'm up and at their door at 0730 tomorrow, breakfast will be a drink of water and a candy bar, since as of 1800 I couldn't find either an MRE or any of the French stuff. GEN Nash's order is that none of us are to have hot meals until we all can, and that may be a month. I have to assume that MREs or some of the French stuff will show up tomorrow. Actually, I left Bad Kreuznach with half a dozen or so MREs in a paper bag and half a dozen bottles of water, but the bag fell under one of the Humvees on the plane and ripped. I was able to rescue only one MRE, which I finished off this morning, and the water bottle I had been nursing—I lost the others.

But I didn't lose any of my luggage—all seven pieces[1] came through fine plus the laptop computer I carried all the way. But I lost my new Army gloves at the control tower today. I have hopes of getting them back, though, since I have COL Patton, the flight line commander, looking for them.

The normal work day at HQ 1 AD seems to start at 0800, at least when it doesn't start at 0500 or 0600, and probably peters out at midnight. At least COL Stratman said I could have the key to the container because he comes in at around midnight and leaves before I do.

Sure wish I'd had the brains to bring a couple of sheets suitable for a sleeping bag. Instead I'm using a couple of towels.

---

[1] Seven pieces because I had a lot of Army stuff and one civilian suitcase I would have, but couldn't leave at HQ 1AD in Bad Kreuznach. Note of 3 January 2003.

The containers aren't bad. I estimate them at 6 feet by 20 and maybe 10 high. Generals get an entire container; colonels, I assume, have one container mate: I saw three beds (a bunk and a bed) in one and I suppose others contain two bunks (four people). They are well lighted and have electric heaters. About 40 feet from me by covered passageway is a container with running water, toilets, showers, and washing-shaving sinks. This morning GEN Cherrie stood beside me shaving and gabbed merrily. A maid mops the floor in the containers every day—a good thing, considering how muddy the streets are.

I'm the only person on the street in American BDUs not wearing a helmet and flak jacket and carrying full equipment. Most are armed, too. The UN people walk around like me.

A Russian Airborne joke: the Russian armed forces were having running, shooting, jumping, etc. competitions. In the running, Army private Ivanov was leading his heat, but collapsed just before the finish. Airborne private Sidorov was carrying a heavy oak door, but just the same led his heat and won it. Afterwards someone asked the Airborne colonel why their guy carried the oak door. "Oh, that's so that in case it looks like he may not win the heat he can drop the door and run even faster." (In the Russian armed forces there are two branches. One is the Navy. The other is almost everything else—Land Forces, Air Forces, Missile Forces, and Airborne Forces—collectively called the Army. In addition, there are Border Forces and Internal Forces, all of which look a lot like the Army and perform most of the same functions. So when the Russians say they've pared their Army down to 1 1/2 million men, that's true, but...)

Thurs 21 Dec 95 2000

Major Lorenz got me a sheet. Sergeant First Class (SFC) Yefimov helped me get a box of a dozen MREs and half a dozen bottles of water, so I didn't depend on the

Russians for supper, but I did for dinner. I spent most of the day with Russian Air Force GEN Denisov.

GEN Viktor Denisov is Deputy Chief of Russian military air transport and his function here is to get data on the airfield and make arrangements for the Russian air transport that will be coming in here in January and thereafter.

GEN Denisov told the following joke: A fellow caught a goldfish, and the goldfish said, "Oh, kind sir, if you'll just let me go, I'll grant you one wish." The fellow said fine, his wish was to find Yugoslavia. The goldfish said OK, first just show me a map. The fellow did, and then the goldfish looked for Yugoslavia. The goldfish looked and looked, but all it could find was Bosnia and Herzegovina, Croatia, and Serbia—no Yugoslavia anywhere. So the goldfish gave up and offered the fellow another wish. All right, says the fellow, make my wife into a beauty. The goldfish said OK, first just show me her picture. The fellow does. "Yipes!" says the goldfish, "gimme the map—I'm going to go look for Yugoslavia some more."

Someone brought in a few of today's *Stars and Stripes*, the first I've seen since Monday's issue at Ramstein plus a bunch of Monday's issues lying around at what are now the former UN HQ, now turned over to us.

Flashes popped and cameras rolled all over the place today. A glimpse of me may or may not appear. The Russians have orders not to give interviews, but when a Russian working for CNN ambushed GEN Denisov walking down the road, the General did say a few words. I was to the General's left; we were on the way from where the Russians are staying to the airfield tower.

We saw a C-17 land and take off and also had a look inside, and I have to say that, whatever troubles the plane has experienced, I think it is a plane the US needs. C-5s can carry the load, but can't land at short strips like Tuzla's. C-130s carry only one third of a narrower and lower load, and I'm sure no variant of a 747 could do the job, either. C-130s are in fact doing the bulk of the carrying here, though. Since

9

the fog lifted this morning, they've been coming in several every hour and going right back out again.

Major Bushyhead, SFC Yefimov, and Russian COL Ashikhmin scouted the area northeast of here today. At one point they saw mines just lying around in the open. They talked to both Muslim and Bosnian Serb soldiers and experienced no difficulties, although there was a rumor that they had. Rumor also has it that Bosnian Serbian GEN Ratko Mladic has given orders to go after the Russians.

GEN Denisov is a politically sophisticated man and has a fairly good notion of what went wrong in Russia and what might be able to fix it. He accepted my argument that the single most important thing is regularly held elections, the results of which are respected.

The phone in the container rings pretty regularly until late at night. Never has it been a call for me or COL Stratman. Yesterday it was mainly Pakistanis; today it has been mainly Americans. Finally I got smart and went to HQ next door for a few numbers. That may or may not help, as there was a lot of uncertainty there about numbers. I had barely written this down, at 2115, incidentally, when I had my first customer, and I've had several since. The number here has been given out as an important one at HQ 1 AD; I'll be lucky if people quit calling before midnight.

COL Patton found my gloves.

An AFN reporter, an Air Force staff sergeant named David Johnson, wanted to interview GEN Denisov, and he looked so stricken when the general had to refuse that I hardly knew what to say.

Friday, 22 Dec 95

The dangerous thing about the mines COL Ashikhmin and Major Bushyhead saw yesterday was that some of them were partially covered by snow, which means that there were others completely covered. They were anti-tank mines, which means there wouldn't have been much left of their Russian jeep if they had hit one.

Today was the first clear day we've seen here. It was even kind of nice for a while.

The Russian group coming by land from Sarajevo finally arrived at about 1400. The head of the group, GEN Staskov, gave an interview to Washington Post reporter Rick Atkinson through me. Atkinson came in with us on GEN Nash's plane last Monday.

It will sure be nice sometime in the evidently not-so-near-future to get away from all of the mud. Then we'll probably curse the dust.

Sooner or later I suppose I'm going to have to face up to washing the...

2115
The Russians asked for an unscheduled meeting so various specialists could talk to their counterparts. It took over an hour and I just got back.

...trousers and shirt I've been wearing since Monday. Altogether I have four sets, but two of them are summer weight.

I hope mail distribution is set up by Christmas. It just about has to be.

This was my 14th day at work in a row. True, I got last Saturday morning off in Bad Kreuznach.

The phone hasn't rung once while I've been here this evening. [Because COL Stratman disconnected it.]

Sat, 23 Dec 95 1000

COL Stratman got off work early last night—he came in at 2215. I was already in bed.

A few minutes later GEN Denisov knocked on the door to invite me to party some with him and some other Russians in the container opposite mine. I begged off as I knew Major Bushyhead was expecting me at work at 0800

11

this morning. About three minutes later GEN Denisov was back and that time I went.

There was a certain amount of socializing and drinking of Yugoslav wine. Then everyone left except GENs Denisov and Staskov and a colonel of theirs who had been here a year and a half as part of the Russian effort and speaks usable Serbo-Croatian, but whose name I never got. There was a certain amount of philosophizing about the fate of Russia. Both Staskov and Denisov, and especially Denisov, had been drinking wine. Staskov believes that first the official Church discredited religion in Russia, then the Soviet leadership discredited Communism, and now the present regime has discredited democracy.

But the real reason I was called over was not all of the above. Denisov had obviously told Staskov that I was someone the Russians could talk to and who might understand what they were saying. It turned out that Staskov had not been happy with his meeting with GEN Nash late in the afternoon at which I had been the interpreter. Now he wondered whether I had any influence with GEN Nash. I could only laugh at that. But what Staskov, who has headed the Russian peacekeeping effort in Bosnia and Herzegovina for three years, wanted me to get across to GEN Nash was his opinion that the Americans here may be making or about to make big mistakes that could lead to terrible trouble. He thinks we don't understand the situation very well and that we can't settle anything by force. He does not think Milosevic runs the show from Belgrade, but that there are other forces here, forces that may be inclined to decisive action to achieve their goals and that flexibility, a word he stressed several times, will have to be manifested by the Americans if the peace is to be maintained and the common cause served. I said that perhaps a rough analogy could be drawn with the American experience in Vietnam, and he agreed that the analogy was apt. I pointed out that GEN Nash does have a political adviser from the State Department on his staff. One more thing Staskov said was that the 1st, 2nd, and 3rd World Wars had all begun in Bosnia.

After I was made an honorary member of the Russian Airborne Assault Forces, the party broke up just before midnight.

Sun, 24 Dec 95 1015

What GEN Staskov said to the Washington Post reporter was that the Bosnian Serbs had given their assent to the Dayton Agreements on the understanding that elements of the Russian Brigade would be stationed in Brcko and the Posavina Corridor, which to them is the Road of Life to the area centered around Banja Luka [BAH-nyah[[LOO-kah], and thereby serve as guarantors of their safety in that area, and now the Russians' mission has been changed in that the area of the Russian Brigade's sector starts to the east of Brcko. COL Ashikhmin had already pointed out to me that since according to the Peace Agreement not a single bullet, much less heavy equipment, is to pass east to west through the Posavina Corridor, the position of the Serbs to the west of it is a disadvantageous one. GEN Denisov and I held a summit meeting on that issue and decided that the solution is the guaranteed permanent (or at least very long-term) stationing of IFOR (Implementation Forces) troops there to guard a two-level passageway, one north-south for the Croats and Muslims, one east-west for the Serbs, to remain there long after IFOR troops have been withdrawn from the rest of Bosnia.

GENs Staskov and Denisov left yesterday morning. COL Ashikhmin completed his recon of an area to place RUS BDE HQ yesterday and left this morning. As I understand it, no more Russians are expected here until after 7 Jan.

COL Ashikhmin told me he voted for the Communists for two reasons: because they are more inclined to measures of social welfare and because he thinks there should be a coherent opposition to those in power. I.e., basically a two-party system. He doesn't favor reversal of the

13

reforms accomplished so far and doesn't think the Communists would try that, anyway. He thinks Zyuganov and crew are a different crowd from the old gang. Let's hope so.

Another GEN Denisov joke, this one from Soviet times:

Two lions, a young one and an old one, were stationed to guard the entrance to Division HQ. And then they were forgotten. Nobody came to relieve them and after several days they were getting pretty hungry. So finally the young one just up and ate the general who commanded the division. "You stupid jerk," the old lion said to the young one. "Now there's going to be hell to pay. You should have eaten the zampolit [zuhm-pah-LEET] (the political officer, the one responsible for Communist Party political propaganda in the division); that way nobody would have ever noticed."

COL Ashikhmin, a full colonel, makes about $400 a month, plus his wife brings in about $40 a month as a kindergarten teacher. He says they live well enough, but there is no way he can save money to buy a car. And they need a car, because they have a little dacha plot to the west of Moscow about two hours by suburban train plus a bus ride. This is a man at least as important as any active duty military person at the Marshall Center.

25 Dec 95 1030

We left Bad Kreuznach about this time a week ago today, but it seems much longer ago.

On Sunday Major Bushyhead had said he might get me up at 0300 or so, so I spent most of Sunday evening sorting out my stuff and packing. Then later he said a taxi would be waiting for me at 0550. I set the alarm for 0515.

At 0605 the phone rang arousing me from a deep sleep. "Jim, where the hell are you!?" I'd set the alarm for PM. By 0645 I was lugging my stuff into 1 AD HQ building

14

at Bad Kreuznach. We left Bad Kreuznach at 0912 and arrived at Ramstein Air Base at 1045. Then we, "we" being three vanloads of lower-ranking people, drove around and around and around trying to find out where the heck we were supposed to be at Ramstein, which is a huge place. Then we found it and were stuffed mainly in the corridors of a small "low-rent" style Air Force building, now including GEN Nash and his immediate entourage, who had come by helicopter from Bad Kreuznach. Mid-afternoon we were told the flight was cancelled due to bad weather. GEN Nash started back to Bad Kreuznach, this time by van because of the weather. The rest of us had our choice. We of the three vans elected to stay at Ramstein. We checked into the guesthouse there and Major Bushyhead and State Department political advisor to GEN Nash Felix Vargas set off for the PX.

At about 1630 I was in the middle of Monday's *Stars and Stripes* when the hotel clerk knocked frantically on the door to say our flight was leaving in an hour and where were Bushyhead and Vargas? I said to page them at the PX.

Anyway, by 1730 we were all at the airfield and our C-130 actually took off at 2000, arriving at TAB at 2230.

C-130s are very noisy inside—passengers wear earplugs. We sat on web seats along the sides between the two Humvees and the pilots' cabin with luggage heaped in the middle. The interiors of C-130s are full of pipes, wires, chains, and all kinds of technical things mounted on the interior walls.

There was a lot of standing around in a drizzling rain on the ramp before Major Lorenz finally got us assigned housing and transported thereto. I think it was about 0200 when I got to bed in my sleeping bag on a real bed. It was OK except I hadn't brought a sheet and none was immediately available.

There is an awful lot of tedium—standing around and/or sitting around and waiting and a lot of rushing hither and thither in an army taking to the field, a lot of

15

disorganization. A worm's eye view would suggest that the Army is run by a bunch of nincompoops.

I think the truth is different.

An army exists to fight its country's wars. War by definition is a non-routine activity. Non-routine means a multitude of low-level decisions being made ad hoc in a general state of near-chaos. I am sure that there are sergeants, lieutenants, captains, and majors here and there who are not very competent, but my general observation is the opposite one—that most of them are highly competent and simply make the best of a very difficult situation.

I realize 1 AD is not going into action in a shooting war—at least that is what we hope. But deploying about 20,000 soldiers and their equipment in the middle of winter onto a territory strewn with mines over bad roads and where the airfield is socked in for days at a time and where there just the same is a real chance of people taking pot shots at you is no simple thing.

So I wish the mud weren't ubiquitous, that we had had hot meals from day one, that the *Stars and Stripes* was delivered daily, that there had been mail in and out the first week, that a PX were set up where I could get this week's *Newsweek*, on which we are the cover story, that a laundry was working, and that Finance was set up so I could claim reimbursement for my travel by train from Garmisch to Bad Kreuznach and for my hotel expenses there. But I understand why much of this is slow in coming.

I left Garmisch in a big hurry Fri, 8 Dec 95.

After my return to Garmisch 30 Nov from the initial meetings at Bad Kreuznach I was trying to take leave and tie up loose ends at FLTCE in the general expectation that I might be recalled to Bad Kreuznach for further meetings with the Russians and then with or without a break be sent on to Bosnia.

On Fri, 8 Dec 95, I was on leave, but dropped by FLTCE Commander Major Chuck Squires' office about 1300. I was barely in the door when the phone rang. It was

16

Major Bushyhead at Bad Kreuznach wanting me at work at HQ 1 AD in Bad Kreuznach at 0800 the next morning. I left Garmisch by train at 2134 and reported for work at 0730 the next morning.

COL Lentsov and his assistant chief-of-staff, LTC Aleksei Alekseyevich Frolov, had arrived Friday and I was really supposed to have been there then, but Major Bushyhead hadn't started trying to reach me until Thursday evening and I had neglected to give him my home phone.

COL Lentsov had adventures, too. The person in a van sent to pick him up at Frankfurt airport Friday failed to connect with him. COL Lentsov and LTC Frolov stood around for 45 minutes and then spotted a U.S. soldier with van obviously waiting to pick up somebody. They assumed it was them and thereby got delivered to Wiesbaden. Eventually it all got sorted out.

There was a 1 AD Christmas party that evening and I'm told my presence would have smoothed things there, too.

COL Lentsov and LTC Frolov were supposed to return to Moscow Wednesday, but didn't actually get away until Thursday.

I expect there will be further mishaps, too.

1545

Not, I'm afraid, a very merry Christmas at TAB and HQ 1 AD. The rains resumed about noon and even pavement is again awash in mud. Christmas dinner involved standing outside in line (the line moved pretty fast, though) to enter a tent on wheels to get ham and turkey (as someone said, which is the ham and which is the turkey?), a soggy mass that may have been spinach, a dollop of something resembling sweet potato, soggy corn on the cob, some beans of some kind, mixed nuts, and a piece of mince pie if there had been a spatula, which you took inside the dining hall to eat. For drinks I had a paper cup of Coke. Oranges and apples were to be had. Early-comers were presented with a bag of candy bars from Mars. No mail call and no *Stars and Stripes* since Thursday or Friday. Most people are on duty, so except for the hot meal it's pretty much like any other day here. I keep reminding myself that I and everyone else here volunteered for this at one time or another.

The UN people were being fed really well at the same dining hall, but I suppose it wasn't possible to continue that because there are so many more of us.

Wed, 27 Dec 95 0910

Yesterday I spent nine hours, from 1000 to 1900, in the right rear seat of a Humvee without getting out. When I did get out, I stumbled some for awhile.

Major Tom Wilhelm, a former FAO (Foreign Area Officer) student at USARI (the United States Army Russian Institute), now the IES (Institute of Eurasian Studies) at the Marshall Center, asked me to go along on a JMC (Joint Military Commission) foray into the Bosnian countryside in case they turned up someone there who could speak Russian. Major Wilhelm is to remain at HQ 1 AD after the Russians come to effect liaison with them from this end.

About eight Humvees set out in a convoy. Three, including the one I was in, had manned machine guns mounted on the roof. The gunner stands in the Humvee with body from the chest up exposed to the whatever. Yesterday was a dreary, very soggy day with rain falling lightly until about 1730. So the gunner's lot is not to be envied.

Our driver on the way out was a young woman about Emily's age [21], blonde and blue-eyed and probably attractive under her helmet, flak jacket, and other gear. On the way back she was the gunner, but had it a little easier because the rain stopped and because she was able to put her back to the wind since on the way back we brought up the rear.

Our goal, it turned out, was a soccer field somewhere north of Tuzla, in Bosnian Serb territory, I think, where we were to set up a mobile radar installation for detection of incoming artillery rounds. This radar can determine practically instantly not only where the shell is going, but also precisely where it has come from, whereupon those who fired it have less than a minute to depart the area before our response arrives [assuming a decision has already been made to respond in this way].

We sat there interminably while the engineers set the radar up and waited until the infantry arrived to set up perimeter guards. For awhile there was talk that we might stay all night, which would have been bad for COL Stratman because I have the only key to our container.

CNN and others filmed the convoy and children waved to us as we went by. Housing looks a lot better than in Russia. From the stalks it looks as though the corn grows a lot taller here.

There was a fair amount of horse-drawn transport. Cabbage seems to be a prime agricultural product. There doesn't appear to be any war damage in the immediate Tuzla area, but as we neared what turned out to be our goal there was a lot. It looked to me like deliberate destruction of housing, but maybe it wasn't. I saw several Muslim minarets and quite a number of Catholic [??] churches.

If the soccer field is in a Serbian area, either it was taken from the other side or is just on the other side of an ethnic border, because all the signs I saw yesterday were in Latin letters, which indicates either a Muslim or a Croat area, since the Serbs use a Cyrillic alphabet mostly identical with the Russian alphabet. [Actually, the Serbs use the Latin alphabet a lot, too.]

The trip was worthwhile for me just to get a look at the countryside even though it was tiring, sometimes uncomfortable, and it turned out there was nothing for me to do. I told my companions for the day that on the basis of this one day's experience I would probably not be able to persuade my daughters to join the Army.

No regular delivery of *Stars and Stripes* yet and no mail yet, either, that I know of.

19

Major Bushyhead does have an office for us now, so I can bring my dictionaries, etc over and work here.

It's snowing today at TAB.

Sent my first mail out today.

Major Bushyhead wants me to go out on recon with him tomorrow to the place where there is a hole in the road twenty feet across and ten feet deep. The hole in the road lies between here and where the Russians want to put their brigade HQ.

Neither the Muslims nor the Serbs want to fix it because each says the other did it. The Russians don't want to fix it because they would have to bring in heavy equipment. Clearly everyone is hoping GEN Nash will say we'll fix it.

Thurs, 28 Dec 95 1350

Major Bushyhead just brought in yesterday's and today's *Stars and Stripes*. My hero.

The expedition to look at the hole in the road has been put off until tomorrow.

Major Bushyhead just brought me in a cup of coffee. A hero thrice over!

A group of fifty Russians are due here 5 Jan to facilitate the arrival of the rest of them. COL Lentsov is to be here the seventh.

Fri, 29 Dec 95 1300

Temperature in the 20's and even teens higher up (in F); snow on the ground and streets and roads are very slick.

We went out and looked at the hole in the road perhaps 15 miles or 25 km east of here.

About two thirds of the way out we entered a hilly but formerly heavily populated area where the war has rendered very nearly 100% of the dwellings unsuitable for habitation. I suppose depopulation, i.e. ethnic cleansing, of the area was the purpose.

The hole in the road is actually at a place where the road is up on the side of a steep hillside, so while the hole may only be 20 or 30 feet across, it is much deeper, essentially all the way down the hill at a point where the road is turning left as you go up. The place is right at the confrontation line, with a tentful of Swedes stationed on the lower, or Bosnian government side, and Bosnian Serbs on the heights above. They could easily have blown us to Kingdom Come had they wished.

We went out and back in a convoy of two British Army Land Rovers up front followed by two Humvees, both with manned machine guns on the roof. I rode front right in the first Humvee. It is GEN Nash's order that no fewer than four IFOR vehicles travel together; this is to enhance security.

The Brits were not wearing helmets or flak jackets and carried only automatic pistols rather than M-16 assault rifles.

One of the Brits said to me that he thought the Americans look too aggressive, which may be off-putting to the local population.

Dialects are alive and well in England. I found one of the Brits practically impossible to understand and the other merely difficult.

1840

Major Bushyhead informs me that the Russian Brigade HQ are to be at Ugljevik [oog-lyeh-veek], which is NE of Tuzla about two thirds or three quarters of the way to Bijeljina [bee-yeh-LEE-nah], well within Bosnian Serb territory. I doubt that it is less than three hours' drive from here even after the hole in the road is fixed or bridged. [It turned out to be about two hours' traveling under adverse conditions and just over an hour under good conditions.]

GEN Nash wanted the Russian HQ nearby, and in fact one of their battalion HQ is to be close, at Simin [seemeen] Han [khan], through which we passed today, but I suspect this was a political decision made in Moscow.

An Army lawyer here pointed out to me that the BDUs as I wear them, that is without helmet and flak jacket, look very much like what many Serbian soldiers wear, so I shouldn't stand out. I'm sure the Russian soldiers won't wear helmets or flak jackets, either. So that leaves Major Bushyhead and any other American soldiers stationed with the Russians to stand out.

Sun, 31 Dec 95

1 AD's first mine casualty was yesterday, as apparently the whole world knew within an hour or so of the incident.

A group of our vehicles was driving up a road they had no business being on and drove onto a section which was mined and which had been reported as mined by the side that put them there. I wouldn't want to be the person who ordered them to go up that road, esp. if it was a captain or major. GEN Nash will flay him (or her) bare.

Fortunately the young man, the driver of the lead vehicle, was not critically injured, although I suppose the injury to his right foot or leg could be permanent. It could have been a lot worse. [3 Jan 96. Major Bushyhead says his flak jacket saved him from abdominal and chest injuries or death therefrom and his Kevlar helmet from head injuries when he cracked his head on something.]

COL Fontenot, commander of 1st Brigade, to be stationed in the NW of our sector, that is the Russians' neighbor to the west, and one of my favorite people in this whole thing, certainly stuck his foot deep in his mouth with his remark about Croatian racism. He was right, of course, but the same could almost certainly be said accurately about virtually everyone in this neck of the woods and not only here, so there's no point in saying it, and especially not publicly. I guess it's not going to force him into retirement, though.

2120

I assume the gunfire that rings out from time to time tonight is celebratory in nature, ringing in the New Year.

Supposedly 98 sacks of mail had come in as of yesterday, but none has gotten to us. And today's Sunday. No *Stars and Stripes*, either. And my radio doesn't work in the container.

Evidently only two things happened today: 1) they finally got the pontoon bridge up over the Sava River, and; 2) the budget battle continues in Washington, which isn't news.

I have a cold and am sneezing all the time, so I wouldn't be good company to anybody, anyway. I think I drove Major Bushyhead out of the office just after noon.

I have read about 60 pages in Mikhail Bulgakov's *Belaya gvardiya* (The White Guards) today, a novel about a family of Russian Army officers in Kiev during the interregnum in 1918-19 between the fall of the Old Regime and the imposition of the New.

Not exactly an upper, either.

A quote, one with portent for our own times: "In its [the anger of the peasants] hands it carried a huge club, with which no new beginning in Russia ever dispenses."

And another: "Holy Russia is a wooden country, poverty-stricken and dangerous, and honor is only a superfluous burden to a Russian."

I hope these sentiments aren't true, but I don't suppose we should count absolutely on it.

Wed, 3 Jan 96 2015

Things looked up today, a lot up, I'd even say.

First, for the first time since Bad Kreuznach I got through directly to Rosemary at the Library. Second, mail came, a whole box full of things Rosemary mailed before Christmas. Actually it had been here several days, but the address I had given Rosemary then wasn't sufficiently detailed. And third, a Russian showed up to do some advance work and even though he speaks pretty good English, still it provides me with things to do and someone interesting to talk to. That twice late in the afternoon I stood just feet from SecDef Perry, Shali, and SACEUR Joulwan, the first time frantically trying to take their picture shaking Captain Sergei Tyulenev's hand with Major Bushyhead's camera, doesn't even count.

My cold seems to be pretty much over, too.

I was a little shocked to learn that my boss, Major Bushyhead, lives in a container with three other officers, and in fact until today there were five of them packed in there. Major Bushyhead says the reason I am so privileged (I share an entire container with a colonel who comes in late—2230 to 2330—and leaves early—before 0700) is because of the PhD tacked onto my name. I didn't ask to be so privileged, but I am grateful.

Thurs, 4 Jan 96 0915

Just from the little walking around I did yesterday I got mud spots practically up to my hip pockets. Today it's in the 20s F with light snow.

Wed, 10 Jan 96 1230

At best I seem to be seeing about two *Stars and Stripes* a week, usually days old.

Thurs, 11 Jan 96 1500

Eleven Russian planes are supposed to land here tomorrow, the first at 1000.

Sat, 13 Jan 96 0650

Eleven Russian planes with over 150 people did arrive yesterday.

Most went well, but there were some sparks late in the day.

COL Lentsov and people struck out in the dark for Ugljevik.

1615

I was introduced to and shook the hand of the President of the United States of America today. GEN Nash took him down the line of brigade commanders and I was next to COL Ashikhmin, head of the Russian Liaison Office at HQ 1 AD, who was standing in for COL Lentsov, RUS BDE Commander. That was about 1400. I must say it was quite a rush.

Earlier, at noon, I spent a few minutes with GEN Nash and took the opportunity to ask whether he would renew my "contract" in June and he said he certainly would if I continue to work as well as I have been.

I'm told I made CNN yesterday. I was standing next to GEN Nash as he welcomed the first two planeloads of Russians.

Tomorrow Major Bushyhead and I go to Ugljevik to begin our stint there at HQ RUS BDE.

There has been a certain amount of drama yesterday and today that I'll try to write about when I get the chance.

Ugljevik Power Station, HQ RUS BDE
Tues 16 Jan 96 0930

The crater in the road between here and Tuzla was bridged by the end of the day Sat, 13 Jan 96, and so our initial trip here was a lot shorter than the one the Russians along with some of our people had Friday night.

The crater is just on the Muslim-Croat Federation side of the Confrontation Line with the Serbs holding the heights to the east. The heights seem to form a natural divide, there at least. To the west on Sunday it was wet and muddy; to the east it was overcast but dry. Our convoy consisted of eight vehicles and about twenty people. On the Muslim side mainly children would wave at us; on the Serb side lots of people did, including soldiers. So maybe we are welcome here.

The distance from Tuzla Air Base is about 40 km (25 miles). We took three hours, but it is doable in two. By helicopter, weather permitting, it's 15 minutes.

In some ways it's a lot better here than at TAB (Tuzla Air Base): not much mud and not crowded. Right now besides us there are about 100 Russians here. But after another 700 or so Russians get set up here at Russian Brigade HQ it may get muddy and crowded.

The Russians put bootblack on their boots every morning and look on us with some disdain in that regard. They also think our weapons look kind of bad. Our response is that their toilet is sanitarily unspeakable aside from it being the bombsight squatter type. [Actually squatter-type toilets are better physiologically and are more sanitary then throne-type toilets.] The building we are in is unheated and the water is cold, cold, cold.

I was a victim of Russian hospitality Sunday night. I don't even remember being brought back, undressed, and put into my sleeping bag. I suppose it was worth it, but I was glad to be told that the no alcohol rule extends to us here, so I shouldn't have to go through that again. Yesterday was pretty bad. The Russians felt bad that they had kind of overdone it with me.

I think the Russian chow hall is actually pretty good.

Russian officers stationed in Bosnia get $1000 a month in dollars; enlisted get $800 [eventually it was determined that both officers and enlisted would get $1000; it was some time before they actually began getting paid and for awhile it was considerably less than they were due].

Now for the drama.

GEN Staskov's stated belief was that the agreement called for four Americans to be stationed at HQ RUS BDE and certainly nothing like 20, most of whom are communications people and some are Special Forces (SF) guys. When on Friday about 1700 he tried to prevent our people from going, GEN Nash summoned him to his office and ripped his hide off. [In particular, GEN Nash pointed out that nowhere in the agreement between Russia and NATO is there any provision for a national support group headed by a general which is to be interposed between the NATO command structure responsible for Bosnia and the command structure of the Russian Brigade in Bosnia.] On the way back to the flight line GEN Staskov grumbled to me that GEN Nash didn't have to respect him, but that he did have to respect the country and that this would not sit well in Moscow. That's what I was reporting to GEN Nash at noon on Saturday. The heck of it was that we screwed up Friday evening and only four Americans actually traveled with the Russian convoy Friday night.

COL Lentsov is between a rock and a hard place because of Staskov. To some extent this is also probably due to the results of the Russian parliamentary elections in December. And it could get worse after the presidential elections in June, assuming they take place. On the other hand, one Russian officer told me that Staskov wasn't even supposed to be here and that he just pushed his way in. That may or may not mean that he is working in concert with someone in Moscow, though. Evidently GEN Nash thinks he can handle Staskov.

There are some internal politics among us here, too.

Wed, 17 Jan 96 0915

So far all water drunk by Americans in Bosnia is imported from Italy or France. We're supposed to use it for brushing our teeth, too, but I think most of us at TAB didn't do that. Here we do, though.

The water from the taps is barely above freezing and no one wants to shower in it. Major Bushyhead considered sending each of us back to TAB about once a week for a shower, but this morning he said we'd be setting up a shower tent.

The comms guys in the room next to me and the Major have an electric space heater, but when the Major and I set one up we just blew a fuse. We don't have a bulb for our light socket, either. [It was like living in a cave.]

Several of the SF guys are sick. At first they thought it was from something they ate at the chow hall, but now they think it's flu the Russians brought from the epidemic raging there.

A reporter for *USA News Today* was here yesterday. Today there are reporters from Agency France Press and the *Los Angeles Times* here. Before that Rick Atkinson from the *Washington Post* was here. I heard that GEN Nash is to be on the cover of *People Magazine*.

The SF people bought disinfectant and cleaning materials in town and I now hear the sound of vigorous scrubbing from down the hall.

Tuzla Air Base
Sat, 20 Jan 96 1030

What the SF guys were sick from was something they brought from TAB. By the end of the day Thursday they had all recovered.

On the other hand, Major Bushyhead was awfully sick Thursday night.

Stars and Stripes reporter Kevin Dougherty (see, for example, p.5 of *Stars and Stripes* for Sat, 13 Jan 96) showed up on our doorstep late Thursday. He drives alone in a right-hand drive British Land Rover. He had been coming up Route Kansas, I think, until he entered an area that looked mined. Generals Cherrie (who lost his right leg below the knee to a mine in Vietnam) and Nash would go ballistic if any American soldier were to do anything even remotely as dangerous as that. Anyway, eventually he made his way to HQ RUS BDE at Ugljevik Power Station and we took him in.

Major Bushyhead got him an interview with COL Lentsov and some picture-taking. It was late by then, so I said he'd better spend the night with us, which he did. I loaned him the two blankets I had "acquired" from my quarters at TAB (Staff Sergeant Aguala, in charge of our comms people, a native of Guam and a marvelous fellow—he always tried to take care of me and it's for sure I needed some taking care of—says that in the Army you never steal, you "acquire"), and he spent the night on a spare cot Major Bushyhead and I have in our room. (The previous occupant was Rick Atkinson of the *Washington Post*, but he had his own sleeping bag.) I'm surprised, but he wasn't cold, even though the room is unheated and the low Friday morning must have been about 20 F. The Major did get us a Coleman kerosene lantern Thursday, and it throws out some heat, but you can't leave it on all night.

On Thursday we learned that GEN Nash would be meeting with GEN Staskov at TAB on Saturday the 20th at 1000 and that I should be the interpreter. The first plan was to send a helicopter for me Saturday morning with a four-vehicle convoy laid on as backup in case of fog Saturday AM. But since Dougherty was driving to Tuzla Friday anyway, Major Bushyhead decided to send me here with him.

Kevin and I left Ugljevik at 0915. We made good time and were in downtown Tuzla, where *Stars and Stripes* has an office-apartment, by 1100.

I think the potholes on the road (we took Route Georgia, the way we had come Sunday the 14th) would rip a wheel off many vehicles, but Humvees and Land Rovers take them pretty well. Good thing, because I don't think Kevin missed many of them. Plus he darts a lot, or maybe Land Rovers are just that way. Plus my Kevlar, even with a T-shirt stuffed in it (more SSGT Aguala advice), was boring

29

a hole in the top of my head and the flak jacket was doing a number on the left side of my back plus from ten or so kilometers east the coal smog in Tuzla is sickening plus breakfast had been some crackers and cocoa that wouldn't dissolve in the water because it was too cold plus I hadn't really gotten my sleep out plus there are new security procedures and it took me half an hour standing holding my sleeping bag and a travel case to get into HQ 1 AD, so by the time I had spent an hour or so with Major Tom Wilhelm and COL Ashikhmin and others and had accomplished some admin work plus I was becoming ever more aware how ripe my T-shirt was and in general how grungy I was plus I sat through an hour-and-a-half briefing, so even though I had had some bread and instant coffee courtesy the Russians and some peanuts and pretzels courtesy Tom Wilhelm, about 1500 I began feeling woozy and sick.

Fortunately, COL Stratman has not been assigned a new container mate, so about 1600 I came back to the container in Sunshine Valley, flopped for about an hour, took a shower (disappointingly lukewarm to cool, however), and put on clean underwear. (I'm still in the BDU shirt through the arm of which President Clinton shook my hand the previous Saturday, though), went to supper at the chow hall, and began feeling a lot better.

I spent the evening reading the *Stars and Stripes* from 13, 18, and 19 January.

This morning I washed my head and shaved in hot water, ambled over to the chow hall for a hot breakfast, and in general have been luxuriating in cleanliness and warmth.

But TAB is no longer home. Home is in Ugljevik.

GEN Sir Michael J.D. Walker, COMARRC (Commander, Allied Rapid Reaction Corps, NATO Commander of Ground Forces in Bosnia), has summoned GEN Nash to Sarajevo today, so GEN Nash's meeting with GEN Staskov is scheduled for later this afternoon.

There is a sensation that High Noon is nigh upon us.

30

The "showdown," like so many are, was anti-climactic. GEN Nash expressed his dismay and confusion regarding the Russians' command and control structure. The previous understanding was that the RUS BDE under COL Lentsov was to be under the operational control of the 1 AD commanded by GEN Nash. Now GEN Staskov comes in, sets up a HQ near the RUS BDE HQ [at Vukosavci [voo-ko-SAHF-tsee], about 10 km from Ugljevik], and announces that he is interposed between COL Lentsov and GEN Nash and that COL Lentsov is even forbidden to contact GEN Nash directly.

In the Russian hierarchy, COL Lentsov was supposed to answer to COL GEN Shevtsov, SACEUR GEN Joulwan's Deputy at SHAPE for the RUS BDE in Bosnia, in parallel, I suppose, to GEN Nash's relationship with GEN Joulwan.

GENs Joulwan and Shevtsov are to be here Thursday, 25 Jan 96, and supposedly matters will be clarified then.

COL Lentsov took me aside Thursday evening to express his embarrassment and chagrin at developments. One Russian officer told me yesterday that he did not think Russian Minister of Defense Pavel Grachev was involved in plotting this. I speculated that other forces might be, though, and he conceded the possibility. After the Nash-Staskov meeting last night, this same officer told me that GEN Staskov has a poor grasp of the situation on the ground here and has been compensating by a lot of bluster about how poorly Ashikhmin, Lentsov, et al, are working.

I found a moment this morning to pass that on to GEN Nash, who to my astonishment asked me what I thought he should do. I could only say that he has the good will of COLs Ashikhmin and Lentsov and I could only suggest he press on as he has been. I did take a minute or two to say that nothing he can do will ever allay the suspicions and dislike of the xenophobic Russian right, and that I suspect Staskov is perhaps a part of that segment of the Russian right that is less vitriolic than, say, Zhirinovsky, but

31

still a part of it. Or perhaps he is merely free-lancing as part of a personal power play.

GEN Nash did not get to Sarajevo after all yesterday because of the weather. GEN Staskov left his HQ at Vukosavci on the Serbian side of the ZOS [Zone of Separation, the former Line of Confrontation] not far from Ugljevik at 1415, but did not reach TAB until almost 1730 because of road conditions (snow). So I was stuck overnight and was supposed to fly back by helicopter at 1000 today. So far that hasn't happened. To complicate matters, GEN Cherrie and GEN Staskov are meeting with the Muslim Commander in the area tomorrow and Major Wilhelm thinks it might be good if I were there. Then on Thursday we expect SACEUR Joulwan and the Russian general at SHAPE COL GEN Shevtsov. So my overnight stay at TAB may stretch to a week. I failed to bring deodorant and none is available here and no spare underwear, either, so I may get fragrant by the end of the week.

More serious is the question of who I work for and where I am to be based. Major Bushyhead is unhappy about my staying on here and asked what I preferred. I answered that that is irrelevant: I go where I'm told to. But after thinking about it, I came to realize that it's not that simple. If Major Bushyhead is my boss and he wants me at Ugljevik, then I should probably make active efforts to avoid diversions like the one tomorrow to interpret for Cherrie and Staskov.

Ugljevik Power Station, HQ RUS BDE
Wed, 24 Jan 96 2200

One exciting thing at the Russian Brigade this evening: an anti-personnel mine was found about 30 feet from where I sit in the room Major Bushyhead and I share. One guess is that it fell off one of several inoperable trucks towed away just before we arrived.

Major Bushyhead says COL Lentsov spotted a mine alongside the road we were driving along in his Uazik [oo-AH-zeek] (Russian Jeep), this afternoon.

I left TAB at 0900 this morning in a convoy with GEN Nash up to a JMC meeting he, COL Fontenot, and COL Lentsov were having with high military leaders of all three Bosnian factions. I returned from there to Ugljevik after that meeting with COL Lentsov and Major Bushyhead.

Fri, 26 Jan 96 0900

The mine was a dud—it had no detonator.

Ice storms greatly hindered movement yesterday and are hindering it today.

The SACEUR—GEN Joulwan—and GEN Shevtsov were supposed to arrive at TAB yesterday, the SACEUR to stay several hours and Shevtsov several days. COL Lentsov rushed off to TAB to meet them in a Russian armored personnel carrier, the kind with eight big wheels on four axles. I went along as interpreter. But Joulwan and Shevtsov never showed.

The Staskov issue is still up in the air. COL Ashikhmin has tried to make the case that GEN Staskov does have a legitimate role to play here. His legitimate role is in legal, technical, and logistical support.

Everyone involved in IFOR sooner or later is to be issued an IFOR ID card, including every soldier in the RUS BDE, about 1500 people. I have one, for example [No. 120001]. And GEN Staskov wants one. COL Ashikhmin thinks GEN Staskov should have one, too, and has been trying to make his case. He asked me for help. I researched the issue and wrote a draft memorandum to Major Wilhelm, who reworked it for COL Ashikhmin's signature to 1 AD Chief of Staff COL John Brown. But as of yesterday afternoon GEN Nash was still stonewalling.

GEN Staskov, incidentally, is always and unfailingly cordial to me.

COL Lentsov is now back in direct contact with GEN Nash.

I was present Monday at the meeting where GEN Cherrie introduced GEN Staskov to the Muslim military commanders in the RUS BDE's AOR (Area of Responsibility). Major Wilhelm and I agreed that it would be appropriate for GEN Staskov's interpreter to interpret at the meeting if he wanted to, which he did. When I said to GEN Staskov that this time I was dumping the job on his interpreter, he said, "About time." (*Pora uzh.*)

We have a steady parade of reporters here. Yesterday it was two photographers from *Newsweek*. Today it's *Stern* (a German news magazine) and a stunning young woman who is a reporter with a Norwegian newspaper. Right now (1430) Major Bushyhead is getting her an exclusive interview with COL Lentsov. She speaks pretty good Russian, so she can do the interview herself.

The worst thing about this job is the nearly constant inconvenience, discomfort, and/or illness. I barely get over one cold and another one starts. This time it spread to my eyes (I rubbed them squinting trying to read the small, imprecise print on a couple of Russian newspapers—I realize I need glasses badly for nearsightedness in one eye and farsightedness in the other). The room I share with Major Bushyhead is cold because although the U.S. Army has been in Europe over half a century, it has yet to tumble to the fact that in Europe everyone uses 220 V, not 110 V. So the space heater provided us is on 110 and it burned out the transformer we had to use. So I'm uncomfortable and sick. We do have a kerosene space heater now, but it throws out too much heat and we have to leave a window open. And we turn it off at night, so it's still cold.

The water is off today, so I haven't shaved or washed my head. I might not have, anyway, because the water is so cold. But with no water, the toilet is virtually unusable, too. At least that's not the Army's fault, but is one of the consequences of the ravages of war.

The Major smokes when he is nervous, which is a lot, and I put up with that, too, since I'm certainly not going to insist on observing Army smoking regulations, assuming they apply, anyway.

In other words, I have resolved to be stoic, but that doesn't mean I like it.

Sat, 27 Jan 96 1115

The Russian airlift through TAB is nearly over and their arrival via train to the railhead at Bijeljina, about 20 km east of here, is well under way.

Yesterday evening I had heard that there have been attempts by Russian soldiers to pilfer things from us.

About 0330 this morning I was woken up and asked to come out into the hall to interpret. Our SF guys had caught a Russian soldier trying to steal MREs from next to their tent about 50 feet from where I sit in our room writing this. This soldier was a real grubby and not very intelligent-looking fellow—I don't expect I looked very prepossessing, either, standing there in my long johns and boots. Our SF fellows, who are a pretty stern group, literally had him collared standing there with his rifle slung around his neck with a hangdog sad sack look. When they asked him why he did it, he muttered the equivalent of "I dunno." They dragged out of him his name and the names of his platoon and company commanders. He pleaded with them not to tell the Brigade Commander because if they did, he'd probably get sent back to Russia and he had just arrived. Someone had gone after the Russian duty officer, who came in at this point and took charge of the soldier, who turned out to be a sergeant. This especially steamed our fellows, all sergeants, who probably don't understand that in the Russian army a sergeant may just be a draftee in his second year of service who hasn't screwed up too badly so far.

Major Bushyhead had slept through all of this—I don't know why he wasn't gotten up, too.

About 0530 a Russian officer came into our room and identified himself as the deputy commander of the soldier's company with responsibility for morale and morals (*vospitanie*). He apologized, said how ashamed they were, promised the soldier would be punished, and asked the Major not to take the matter to COL Lentsov, to which the Major agreed.

GEN Staskov is moving his HQ to Ugljevik. GEN Nash told Major Bushyhead to tell COL Lentsov not to worry about it. [It never happened.]

COL Lentsov did not appear at 0730 for the regular morning conference call with GEN Nash nor could we get any straight story on where COL Lentsov was.

Later in the morning Major Bushyhead had an unsettling experience.

The Major came out of a building to find himself confronted by an angry-looking COL GEN Shevtsov, who wanted to know why the Major had not had the courtesy to meet a three-star general upon arrival. The fact of the matter was that COL Lentsov had failed to notify Major Bushyhead of the COL GEN's impending arrival, but the Major took the hit for COL Lentsov, saying he had made a big mistake and it wouldn't happen again. All this in the presence of cameras and reporters. [The reporter from *Stern* got a magnificent shot, which Major Bushyhead later didn't know whether to be proud of or chagrinned about.]

GEN Shevtsov then blustered on, demanding to know why there are so many Americans here and in particular the SF guys, but not waiting for an answer. [GEN Shevtsov was probably doing this for political effect at home, because throughout, to the best of my knowledge, he has been fine to work with and is certainly friendly to Americans, including me.]

Major Bushyhead has reported all this directly to GEN Nash.

The German reporter from *Stern*, whose Russian is good, also gave me the essential details of the dressing-down

Major Bushyhead got from COL GEN Shevtsov for not meeting him this morning. The only detail the Major had omitted from his report to GEN Nash was that he was in the company of the gorgeous Norwegian reporter when Shevtsov spotted him.

1400

I'm a little concerned about something else.

The Jan 15 issue of *Time* magazine has an article about how the United States plans to help the Bosnian Muslims achieve military parity with the Bosnian Serbs in training and equipment. The plan is that the U.S. will pay private contractors, many of them prominent retired American military officers, to do the job.

If and when this begins to happen and it begins sinking in on the Serbs that it is happening, I doubt that the Serbs, or at least all Serbs, will react to it with equanimity.

I agree that the Bosnian Muslims should have military parity with the Bosnian Serbs. My concern is what the consequences may be for the American military in Bosnia and specifically for us here at Ugljevik with the Russians.

Force protection is at or near the top of the list of GEN Nash's priorities. All American bases are heavily guarded, traveling is by armed convoy, etc. But that's for Americans serving with Americans. So far, at least, the Russian camp at Ugljevik is completely open and unguarded. Anyone can wander in. A small forest begins on a hill about 40 feet from our window. We Americans occupy the three end rooms of the building and a tent a few feet away plus several tents across the river (the Janja [YAH-nyah]). All this is easily pin-pointed. If a night attack were mounted, it should be possible to slaughter us all or take us hostage with little or no resistance.

I have to assume that someone is taking this into account.

1530

Captain Hedin says our three rooms are not quite as vulnerable as I had imagined because of the SF guys in their tent next door and because the Russians do post guards, only not a full perimeter defense, but the guys across the river are very vulnerable because a main highway runs right past them. He notes that we here are in violation of most of GEN Nash's force protection guidelines. So I guess I have to hope the SF guys don't get sent home any time soon. Besides which, they are great at catching pilferers.

2000

This time the Major was the victim of hospitality, in this instance a double whammy of Russo-Serbian "hospitality" that apparently went on most or all of the afternoon. It's a tough situation to be in—official orders are that we are not to do it, but when invited to an official function I don't see how it can be avoided.

I expect each and every one of us here sacrifices a certain amount of his or her health to the cause.

For example, the area is probably pretty polluted if only because of the power station—at least the smell of coal is pretty strong sometimes, especially early in the morning.

Sun, 28 Jan 96 1100

Wednesday after the Joint Military Commission (JMC) meeting with the military leaders from the three Bosnian factions, which took place near the HQ of 1st Brigade 1 AD, commanded by COL Gregory Fontenot, COL Fontenot invited COL Lentsov to his quarters.

COL Fontenot says his career is over because of his remarks about Croatian racialism and that he is staying on here until this is finished just because of his soldiers. Major Bushyhead says the only reason Fontenot wasn't relieved was because of the support he got from all of his people. Fontenot is pretty bitter and it was pretty emotional.

He was briefing his soldiers on what to expect in Bosnia when he made his unfortunate remarks and a reporter just happened to be present who broadcast them to the world out of context.

It's all pretty sad.

1150

A few minutes of excitement. COL GEN Shevtsov just dropped by. He was entirely cordial to the Major, used the familiar form of address, and promised he would instruct Lentsov to set the Major up with an office at the Russian Brigade HQ building. The biggest flap came from someone concluding we need a bucket after observing Captain Hedin using water bottles to flush the toilet.

29 Jan 96 1100

The big flap today is that COL GEN Shevtsov, who took a brief look at our quarters yesterday, told GEN Nash at dinner last night that Bushyhead (and presumably Nelson) is (are) living in hygienically unsanitary conditions and this morning during the telephone conference GEN Nash told the brigade commanders and everyone else listening about Shevtsov's remarks. The Division Sergeant Major (that's SM Tilley, the one who won fame keeping the troops entertained 13 Jan while waiting for the President) is supposed to visit us this afternoon and Major Bushyhead says he'll be damned if he'll sweep the floor of our room before he comes. Anyway, that's why I asked for a whisk broom and dust pan when I talked to Nika this morning (actually, I had been thinking about it already). [GEN Shevtsov was right; the place was VERY unsanitary.]

1600
The SM didn't show today.

Sometime yesterday evening COL Lentsov asked us to have a low-boy trailer truck at the Bijeljina railhead today at 1500 to transport two forty-ton bulldozers to Priboj [pree-boy], a few km down the road from us towards Tuzla. Major Bushyhead was on the phone all morning working it, having begun the night before. He got the intervention of two generals and disturbed rafts of colonels, majors, and lessers all to make it happen today instead of tomorrow. We were on the verge of setting out to go get the truck and escort it to Bijeljina when we unexpectedly learned that not only had the train with the bulldozers not yet arrived in Bijeljina, it was unclear when it would. Major Bushyhead is sure his name is Mudd throughout most if not all of 1 AD over this. I suggested that we should seek more precise information next time we get such a request and said he shouldn't take it too deeply to heart.

Tues, 30 Jan 96 1100

Now the train is expected at 1500 today. We have two trucks ready to leave from 1st Brigade, in the NW of the American sector, but this time nothing will happen until we get word that the train with the bulldozers has actually arrived.

Fri, 2 Feb 96 0900

GEN Nash paid his first visit to Russian Brigade HQ Tues, 30 Jan 96. The Russians put on a pretty good meal for him at a mobile field kitchen/dining facility. I drank one "symbolic" shot of vodka, "symbolic" amounting to maybe an American double shot.

GEN Staskov spoke for the Russians and sounded entirely conciliatory.

NBC or CBS, I'm not sure which, was here that day.

From 1930 that evening until 0330 Wednesday morning I barfed three times and slept poorly.

40

Nevertheless, at 0715 Wednesday I was at Russian Brigade HQ for the daily morning telephone conference and at 0800 left with COL Lentsov and Major Bushyhead to travel west to Celic [CHEH-leech] to meet with the American LTC [LTC Anthony Cucolo] from our 1st Brigade who has been manning a checkpoint and patrolling an area in the Russian AOR (Area of Responsibility) until the Russians can get set up.

Every time I think that surely the worst is over, it gets worse.

I was thoroughly miserable all morning and by the time LTC Cucolo had finished briefing COL Lentsov I was completely at the end of my tether. If it had gone on any longer, I would have collapsed.

Last Wednesday afternoon NBC (or CBS?) did an interview with COL Lentsov that was thoroughly wooden and my translation even more wooden.

Thursday morning I was up for the morning telephone conference, but otherwise pretty much packed it in for the day. I did translate the interview Lentsov gave *Ogonyok* for their issue N.3 in January. GEN Nash gave a dinner at TAB for all his brigade commanders and I was to have gone as interpreter, but the Major begged off for me. The Russians provided an interpreter, but I don't know who or how it went.

I feel all right today.

I took my last shower two weeks ago Tuesday. I haven't had the courage to face the ice water of the shower here yet. I can barely stand to wash my hair.

Most of humanity for most of its existence, of course, has lived and lives under conditions closer to these than to the ones I am used to.

The only event of note so far today are some petty and unsubstantiated complaints the Bosnian Muslims have about the Russians.

The wrap-up on the lowboy and the Russian bulldozer is that we sent two lowboys, but for some reason one of the bulldozers made its own way from Bijeljina to Priboj.

The Russians have greatly bucked up security at their HQ this morning.

The American lieutenant who stepped on a mine yesterday and lost a foot was blown into the air and came down on an anti-tank mine, which might have gone off if the lieutenant had been heavier. This was in an area which was supposedly clear of mines.

Three of our artillery guys are being withdrawn. Three SF guys have already left and an MI guy may go. On the other hand, we are gaining a FAO (Foreign Area Officer) major with Russian capabilities and may gain two. These are people on 179-day TDYs (TDY: temporary duty) from the Marshall Center in Garmisch.

1515

Two Russian reporters were just here and got a good interview from the Major. It helped that I was in good form.

Mon, 5 Feb 96 0900

1 AD has had its first [and, as it turned out, only] fatality from a mine. The sniping in Sarajevo is a little disquieting, too.

I should have a brief spot or two on Russian Channel Two TV tomorrow and/or the next night.

I think the Russians, the officers at least, are doing a better job of putting their living areas in order than we are. Efforts are being made by both the Russians and the Americans to improve our standard of living and also force protection.

The time, effort, and money spent in November and December wining and dining important members of COL Lentsov's team and COL Lentsov himself at Bad Kreuznach were extremely well spent because the result was the establishment of personal relationships and trust, without which this would be a terribly difficult operation to conduct. I feel this personally as time and again I have to run down the answer to some question and it is just so much easier if I can turn to someone I already know and then go on from there to build new relationships.

1745

The Russians have a saying: beer isn't vodka—you can't drink much of it.

Thurs, 8 Feb 96 0820

There has been a lot of snow the past three days, complicating travel, esp. since no one plows the roads.

Tuesday we went to TAB to meet COL GEN Yevgeny Podkolzin, Commanding General, Russian Airborne Forces, and to see off GENs Popov and Bespalyi, commanders of the two airborne divisions from which the Russian Brigade in Bosnia was formed. Popov and Bespalyi had been visiting. I liked both of them.

Podkolzin is actually staying not at Ugljevik, but at Staskov's HQ in nearby Vukosavci. Staskov's digs there are a lot better than Lentsov's at Ugljevik—it looked like a vacant ski resort to me. And the Major and I were given a really good supper, which was nice, since we had missed dinner.

Yesterday we went back to TAB to meet Russian Minister of Defense Grachev and SACEUR Joulwan.

The trip to TAB was scary because the road was very slick, the driver appeared to be an inexperienced nineteen-year-old draftee, Lentsov kept hectoring him, and I thought sure we'd go off the road. Russian Uaziki (Jeep-like vehicles) don't have seatbelts and I was wishing mightily I had put on my flak jacket, which might at least save some ribs as I flew over the front seats, not to mention fragments from a mine the vehicle would be likely to hit as it went off the road.

1415

Major Bushyhead is supposed to stick close to COL Lentsov, but Lentsov keeps getting away from him. And yesterday Lentsov had Bushyhead come back with the convoy rather than by helicopter with the rest of us.

I think in part at least COL Lentsov is concerned that if Major Bushyhead is always on him like a leech, and Bushyhead after all is GEN Nash's personal emissary to Lentsov, it will look as though Bushyhead is Lentsov's nanny and that Nash is keeping Lentsov on a short string. National pride, in other words, is at stake.

GEN Nash wanted Russian Brigade HQ close to 1 AD HQ at TAB, probably at Simin Han, but the Russians chose Ugljevik, much further out and in Bosnian Serb territory. And I think they were right to do so. Regardless of internal political arrangements, no large sovereign state should be or be perceived to be following the policies of some other state rather than its own policies. If it is, sooner or later it will be successfully challenged from within and lead to a worsening of relations between the two states. And such a perception, if not the reality, would have been inevitable if Russian Brigade HQ were close to 1 AD HQ at TAB. This is the reason, too, for the Russian sensitivity to the number of Americans stationed at Ugljevik.

This is an entirely different thing, I think, than the question of trust and close and cooperative working relations on a lower, everyday working level. Now that ideology no longer interferes (I mean since the collapse and discrediting of Soviet Communism in Russia), I haven't seen at lower levels any evidence of the old suspicions and fears since the beginning of our mutual undertaking in Bosnia. Sometimes our practices and expectations are different, but I personally don't believe that there have been any walls of distrust that needed knocking down.

Conceivably I'm wrong, at least in relation to this or that concrete individual, but I don't think so.

There are now three American majors stationed at Ugljevik. All speak Russian to a greater or lesser extent.

John Bushyhead is in charge overall. Tom Wilhelm is going out with the Russians for their interactions with the Bosnian Serb (and presumably also Muslim and Croat) military authorities. Major Richard Choppa came from the Marshall Center in Garmisch on a 179-day TDY—I don't know what is in store for him after that.

His area is primarily internal issues—intra-American and Russo-American.

Majors Jeff Stimson and John Cecil, like Choppa, are from the Marshall Center, but are currently at TAB.

Major Choppa is a pretty good barber.

The Russians are all here now, have established their base camps, and are beginning to exercise their peace enforcement responsibilities. Primarily that means patrolling the Zone of Separation (ZOS) and manning twelve checkpoints in it.

Sat, 10 Feb 96 0930

The Bosnian Serbs are mad at IFOR because the Muslims arrested a couple of their high-ranking military people in Sarajevo a few days ago. It is unclear what the consequences will be.

My routine at Ugljevik on days I don't leave Ugljevik is pretty much this: up at 0630 or a little earlier, cold-water hair wash and shave, come in to the office by 0715, take the call and interpret at 0730 when GEN Nash has his conference call with brigade commanders, do whatever all day long until as late as 2030 or even 2100, sometimes with a break of a couple of hours and sometimes not, and to bed. Breakfast is cold cocoa and crackers, lunch and supper usually heated MREs, meals nearly always taken at work. The Army in the field doesn't recognize weekends or holidays. Today differed only in that at 1430 we left by helicopter for TAB and returned about 1930. It's a 15-minute flight. It is 2030 as I write this.

Sun, 11 Feb 96 1600

The trip to TAB yesterday with the Major and COL Lentsov was so that Lentsov could see off the departing COL GEN Podkolzin and GEN MAJ Staskov and so that GEN Nash could meet GEN LT Aleksei Alekseyevich Sigutkin, who is Staskov's replacement.

Mon, 12 Feb 96 0800

Yesterday afternoon a civil affairs and psychological operations (psyops) group came out from TAB to talk to the Russians. Our people publish a weekly newspaper in Serbo-Croatian for distribution to the local population and also handbills, etc. COL Lentsov said the local authorities may or may not be well informed on the IFOR mission, but the local population certainly is not.

GEN Sigutkin was at the briefing. He seems perfectly fine to me. It's interesting that Staskov, whose rank equates to our brigadier general (one star), was replaced by a major general equivalent (two stars). That makes him GEN Nash's equal in rank, which I expect was the idea. He is evidently going to be a lot easier to deal with, but it is still unclear to me, at least, where his position fits in, since at the talks at Bad Kreuznach at the end of November nothing was mentioned of any Russian military structures in Bosnia other than the RUS BDE commanded by COL Lentsov and a liaison group at HQ 1 AD at TAB.

Just before GEN Staskov left, COL Lentsov told me that it was too bad things had gotten off to such a bad start, that GEN Staskov really wasn't such a bad guy, and that GEN Nash had shot from the hip ("swung his saber from the shoulder").

Tues, 13 Feb 96 1530

Early this afternoon Major Bushyhead, COL Lentsov, GEN Sigutkin, and I flew mainly the Muslim side of the ZOS in the Russian AOR. We found a tank in the open and four armored vehicles under cover that shouldn't have been there according to the terms of the Dayton Agreements. We flew in a U.S. Army UH-60 Blackhawk helicopter escorted by an AH-64 Apache attack helicopter.

1930

Stars and Stripes are still few and far between. For example, Major Wilhelm on a trip to TAB today managed to bring back only last Saturday's and Sunday's issues.

Wed, 14 Feb 96 1600

A Russian joke:

This fellow was big and hefty, too big and hefty, he thought, so he went to a doctor to see if there wasn't some way he could lose weight. The doctor gave him some pills, but warned him not to take too many at a time. But the fellow disregarded the doctor's instructions and took all the pills at once. The result was that he lost an awful lot of weight and ended up with lots of loose, left-over skin. So he went back to the doctor to see what could be done. The doctor pulled the fellow's skin up all nice and tight and stored the excess on top of the fellow's head. So the fellow ended up with his bellybutton up on his forehead. "What the heck is this?" "Well, look at it this way," the doctor said. "Now you have a very nice necktie."

Fri, 16 Feb 96 0900

British GEN Sir Michael J.D. Walker, COMARRC (Commander, Allied Rapid Reaction Corps), visited Wednesday afternoon.

Yesterday I went with COL Lentsov and Major Bushyhead to downtown Tuzla for Lentsov's first meeting with the commander of the Bosnian 25th Division. Three-way interpreting was necessary: the Bosnian commander's interpreter did Bosnian (Serbo-Croatian)-English, and I did Russian-English. The meeting, which lasted about an hour, was entirely cordial.

After that we went to TAB, where Lentsov had to attend an interminable meeting of brigade commanders. I whispered translation into his ear as best I could.

While we were gone, the general who commands the U.S. Army's Special Forces visited here. While leaving, one of their helicopters flew over and blew down a bunch of our tents and did some other damage. Our people are pretty mad.

1600

Majors Wilhelm and Bushyhead and I attended the first Russian-hosted JMC meeting today at CP 39, the Russian checkpoint at the top of the mountain pass between here and Tuzla. The Bosnians attending included the 25th Division commander we met with yesterday in Tuzla. The Serbs boycotted the meeting because of the arrest of two of their people in Sarajevo recently. This time the only interpreting I did was some whispering in Major Bushyhead's ear. The meeting was chaired by GEN Sigutkin, who introduced himself as chief of the "gruppa upravleniya," which Major Bushyhead translates as the "operational control group."

Sat, 17 Feb 96 0800

Stars and Stripes correspondent Kevin Dougherty came out yesterday in hopes of getting a short second interview with COL Lentsov. Kevin asked for 15-20 minutes; Lentsov said he'd give him 5 to 10. Lentsov came in to our office for the interview just after 1900 and stayed until 2005. That's far more than Lentsov has given to any other non-Russian correspondent, to the best of my knowledge. And he invited Kevin back when Kevin returns to Bosnia in June or July. So Kevin really struck it rich and now it just remains to be seen how much of what Kevin wants to write will actually appear in the paper. [This interview formed the basis of a large article published in the Sunday supplement to the *Stars and Stripes* on 2 June 96.]

Mon, 19 Feb 96 0900

Thought I was going to have a warm- or hot-water hair wash this morning because the Russians have fixed the hot-water heater in the shower room in our building. The water was heated, but would only drip. I'm pretty much used to cold-water hair washing, anyway. It would be nice to shower there, though. Once again I'm well into my second week without a shower.

Major Bushyhead evidently ate something that didn't agree with him at the Russian mess at Simin Han yesterday and is in terrible trouble today. I ate there, too, but not much because I had to interpret.

Saturday COL Fontenot came over from 1st Brigade to see COL Lentsov and have lunch. GEN Sigutkin (the new commander of the Operational Group at Vukosavci, GEN Staskov's replacement) was present, too. It was all very cordial, good feelings all around.

Yesterday the Major and I traveled with COL Lentsov to Simin Han to meet with GEN Nash.

We have a footbridge up now between HQ Russian brigade and our comms and other people on the other side of the creek. We call it "the Bridge Over the Elba."

1130

The Major tried to give me most of the morning off, but that only lasted about an hour—long enough to do some cold-water laundry in a bucket and a couple of other minor things.

1155

CBS headed by Bob Morton has just arrived.

Thurs, 22 Feb 96 0800

At the telephone conference yesterday morning GEN Nash said to COL Lentsov, pointedly, I thought, "I'll expect you and Jim to supper tonight." I infer that GEN Nash had not been entirely satisfied with the interpreter who substituted for me at the last dinner GEN Nash gave for brigade commanders. So it's nice to have such a vote of confidence.

Two days before, at Simin Han, I had irritated GEN Nash with my coughing, which at that point I hadn't tried treating and which was irritated by GEN Nash's cigar just under my nose.

At the Simin Han meeting GEN Nash told COL Lentsov that it was improper for GEN Sigutkin to chair JMC meetings because he is outside the chain of command. Lentsov said he was sure GEN Sigutkin would understand once that was explained to him and would comply.

COL Lentsov's position is that IFOR should stick strictly to impartial enforcing of the military provisions of the Dayton peace agreement and leave everything else, including the search for war criminals, to the respective competent authorities.

He thinks a big propaganda campaign on the merits of peace should be mounted among the civilian population.

COL Lentsov does not expect resumption of war this year by the official three parties to the Bosnian conflict, but he thinks there is a high probability of terrorism and guerrilla war.

Lentsov got so mad at his driver yesterday for something stupid he did that he smacked him on the back of the head.

Bosnia is a God-awful dismal place in February. Even paved roads are gritty and muddy.

Our footbridge over the river didn't last long. A big log came floating down and hit a support.

On the way to supper with GEN Nash I went into his bathroom facilities to wash my hands. The place was heated, sparkling clean, and with hot water. Thirty seconds of bliss!

Mon, 26 Feb 96 0850

Friday, 23 February 96 was Russian Armed Forces Day (literally: Defender of the Fatherland's Day). It used to be Red Army Day and commemorates the founding of the Red Army 23 Feb 1918.

GEN Nash and 1st and 2nd Brigade 1 AD COLs Fontenot and Batiste were invited to the celebrations.

A banquet-concert began at 1400 and was pretty well over by 1700, by which time most participants (not, thank goodness, including me) were feeling no pain.

Both GEN Sigutkin and COL Lentsov were there, although basically it was Lentsov's show. There was lots of good feeling all around. This in spite of the recent Russian elections, reflected, for example, in the fact that the Russian contingent at the Marshall Center's five-month classes has been reduced from six to two for the Feb-June 96 class.

The only flap had to do with two female American Army officers, a captain and a 1st lieutenant, whom the Russians invited, brought here, and put up for the previous night and prospectively for Friday night, too.

Suddenly, mid-way through Thursday evening we were required to foist a chaperone upon them and when on Friday evening GEN Nash learned they were still here, he dispatched two helicopters to snake them out of here.

It was all unnecessary: the women were having a good time and were adequately watched over. Major Bushyhead and I went into lengthy explanations about the new political correctness in America and how heads roll at the highest military levels over the slightest indiscretions. It ended up with the Russians apologizing to us, which I assured them was not necessary, quite the contrary.

The chaperoning, though, was probably a good idea.

Saturday Major Bushyhead and I went out with LTC Syrtsov, CO of Russian 2nd Battalion in Simin Han, to visit LTC Anthony Cucolo, his counterpart to the north. That's the Celic—Brcko area.

The destruction of housing in SW Brcko is appalling—seemingly square mile after square mile of nearly total destruction. This is from the battles in 1992.

It was a good get-acquainted trip for Syrtsov and Cucolo. They are to set up joint patrolling of Brcko, an especially sensitive area. Before the war the majority of the population was Muslim, but they have been killed or driven out and the city is now in Serbian hands. The Croats are nearby, too.

A BBC crew was filming a documentary out in LTC Cucolo's area and filmed us furiously.

On the way back we took a mountain road for miles that I'm pretty sure is not on our list of cleared roads. It was steep, narrow, and deep in ice and snow. We had no problems, however, unlike the CBS camera crew who covered Friday's festivities and who managed to turn over their Range Rover on straight and level road a few kilometers from here on the way to Priboj. One of the crew broke some ribs and there were some other injuries, but nothing terribly serious, I believe.

Yesterday, like today, the sun was shining. Mid-morning the Major told me to take the rest of the day off. This enabled me to get in on a shower session at the Russian facility, my first shower in seventeen days (I may have missed an opportunity a week or so ago, though). I turned in one set of BDUs to the Russian laundry and later did some light laundry at our digs.

I am told that the Army does in fact have a source of highly qualified interpreters—OSIA (the On-Site Inspection Agency). So I have told Major Bushyhead that if a qualified replacement can be gotten for me when my current TDY ends in June, then that should be done. Six months in Bosnia is enough.

I still have a persistent cough.

1800

A Russian vehicle hit a mine this afternoon. No one was hurt.

The Major was able to arrange Lentsov a telephone call with Lentsov's 16-year-old son, who is in Honolulu on a round-the-world cruise on the Russian sailing ship "Kruzenshtern."

The "Kruzenshtern" is a tall ship, something like the Yankee Clippers of nearly two hundred years ago. The Russian Navy keeps the "Kruzenshtern" as a training ship.

Wed, 28 Feb 96 0800

The Russian vehicle that hit a mine was a light armored personnel carrier on tracks. It hit an antitank mine on a road that supposedly had been checked for mines and had been traveled a lot. The explosion blew off one track and two rollers. The crew was sitting up high and so the worst injuries were a few bruises.

Yesterday afternoon COL Lentsov and I were taken by helicopter to Vlasenica [VLAH-seh-nee-tsuh] to meet with GEN Nash, COL Batiste, and Serbian MAJ GEN Tolimir, evidently Number Two in the Bosnian Serb military structure after Mladic and the one who failed to appear at the Rome conference.

After that we went to COL Batiste's HQ nearby, which although it is located on a hilltop is muddy as all get out by the end of the day.

1030

The phone's been ringing off the hook all morning. Felix Vargas, GEN Nash's political adviser, was supposed to arrive here at 1000 by helicopter, from where he and the Major will travel to Bijeljina to meet the mayor, chief of police, and important business people. About 0930 there was a call to say the helicopter would be delayed due to weather although the weather is fine both here and at TAB. The helicopter landed about five minutes ago.

At the same time GEN Sigutkin and COL Lentsov wanted help and advice in dealing with the failure by the Muslims to declare all their weapons sites in the 10-kilometer zone that runs along the Zone of Separation. The Major called HQ 1 AD and an approach was worked out. The Russians prefer a soft line, we prefer a hard line. A compromise was reached: give the Muslims until 1 March to comply and afterwards destroy any weapons found at undeclared sites. Later it turned out that the problem was not willful non-compliance, but resulted from IFOR working from maps onto which information provided by the FWPs (Former Warring Parties) had been transposed with some inaccuracies.

The intel people hold a telephone conference every day at 1000. Previously when I have been here I have interpreted. Today other things kept coming up, so we made a Russian interpreter do it. He was reluctant because the line is so bad and afterwards he came to me and said we'd apparently decided he would just have to sink or swim. And we had. No interpreter is ever totally adequate, anyway.

1130
Helicopters are here again and the Major just poked his nose in the door. So his schedule with the polad (political adviser) is seriously out of kilter.

1140
Admiral Leighton Smith, IFOR Commander, is coming tomorrow, and his advance people are here poking around. I guess the second set of helicopters was them.

54

1500

COL Ashikhmin told me a week or so ago that in fact tensions were pretty high the first couple of weeks he and his group were working at HQ 1 AD (mid- and late-January), but that now they are perfectly comfortable with the Americans and evidently the Americans with them. So maybe Major Bushyhead is right in telling all and sundry about the walls that needed breaking down.

The Marshall Center says they will support me, but they need a decision within the next two weeks as to whether I am coming home in June for good or whether I am going to stay on here to the end (presumably by the end of the year). I expect GEN Nash to flatter me and appeal to my sense of duty and I expect I will answer that call.

Thurs, 29 Feb 96 0830

The area where the Russian APC (armored personnel carrier) hit a mine on Monday was marked as mined on materials we had given the Russians, but which they apparently had not examined closely.

Fri, 1 Mar 96 0800

Yesterday could have been called "Generals' Day at Ugljevik." Four-star Admiral Leighton Smith, IFOR Commander, came in the morning and four-star GEN Jamerson, Deputy SACEUR, accompanied by two other generals and GEN Nash, came in the afternoon.

The Marshall Center may be deriving some benefit from having me and a number of FAO students here. Admiral Smith asked me where I was from and I replied, "The Marshall Center." He said, "Fine place," and recommended to COL Lentsov that he should go there at least for a look.

After all the visits were over, GEN Sigutkin and COL Lentsov invited me to dinner at their VIP dining facility. We talked about presidential politics and Russian literature. [GEN Sigutkin and I hit it off awfully well.]

Sat, 2 Mar 96 0800

Fri, 1 Mar 96 was the 1st anniversary of the founding of the Bosnian 25th Division and the 3rd anniversary of the Bosnian declaration of independence from Yugoslavia. A parade was held at a stadium in Tuzla to mark the occasion and after a dinner for selected guests, among whom were GEN Cherrie from 1 AD and GEN Sigutkin and COL Lentsov from the Russian Brigade. Major Bushyhead and I were there as straphangers with the Russian Brigade.

The most significant thing seemed to be a long and apparently amicable discussion between the Bosnian generals and the Russians. This is because the Bosnian Muslims have been wary of the Russians and have been coming up with all sorts of petty and mainly spurious complaints against them.

The Russians' Serbo-Croatian to Russian interpreter is a Serb hired locally.

Mon, 4 Mar 96 0945

Saturday, 2 Mar 96, COL Lentsov, COL Lentsov's Serbo-Croatian to Russian interpreter, Major Bushyhead, and I traveled to Celic on the Muslim side and on the way back to Lopare [loh-pah-reh] on the Serbian side for visits to their respective police chiefs and town council chairmen (mayors).

COL Lentsov got them to agree to coordinate activities and even meet under his auspices. A major problem that needs coordinating, for example, is of people wanting to visit the houses they used to live in, but which are now on the other side of the line of separation. IFOR is not supposed to provide escort services, but can facilitate meetings of local officials from both sides and coordination of their activities.

I thought COL Lentsov was awfully good at his diplomatic exercises and told him later that only one Nobel Peace Prize would be insufficient reward for his efforts.

COL Lentsov consistently referred to himself as part of IFOR, making practically no references to the Russia Brigade as such, and made frequent mention of GEN Nash.

On the way back I twisted a muscle in my back and by evening was in very considerable pain, which lasted all night and into yesterday.

Thurs, 7 Mar 96 0900

Tuesday morning GEN Sigutkin and COL Lentsov called me and Major Bushyhead into Lentsov's office, where Sigutkin made a lengthy and very formal statement to the effect that some unknown U.S. Army official for unknown reasons had excluded Sigutkin and his group and also several people in COL Ashikhmin's liaison group at TAB from the list of people eligible to receive IFOR ID cards and demanding to know why.

The Major made a quick phone call to COL Brown, GEN Nash's Chief of Staff, and got the answer that it is COL Lentsov and no one else who decides which of the Russians serving in Bosnia receive IFOR ID cards.

So it all turned out to be a misunderstanding, and a situation where some pretty hard feelings could have resulted was averted.

Tuesday afternoon GEN Sigutkin, COL Lentsov, Major Bushyhead, and I visited the Chairman (Mayor) of the Celic City Council again and afterwards went to a gathering of local notables at a restaurant in Celic. After considerable speechifying and arranging for cemetery and other visits in Serbian-held territory, we had dinner.

I think the Muslims are a pretty sad group of people who have suffered and are suffering tragedy and hardships not for the most part of their own making. The question remaining in my mind is to what extent that is also true of the Serbs.

The Serb who interprets for the Russians used to live in Lukavac [LOO-kah-vahts], near Tuzla, and met someone he knew at this gathering. They seemed glad to see each other.

This Serb has had to flee with his family twice: first from Lukavac and more recently from Sarajevo. Before the war he taught Russian in high school.

GEN Sigutkin told the gathering the following story: a couple of years ago Sigutkin was in Sarajevo and was talking to an elderly Serbian man. The man pointed up the hill to a half-ruined house and said that that was where he used to live. The house next to it was also half-ruined and Sigutkin asked whose house it had been. "Oh, that was my neighbor's house—he's a Muslim." Sigutkin then asked the old man if the Muslim had been a bad neighbor, to which the old man replied, "Oh, no, he was a fine neighbor. He helped me build my house." "Then why did you go to war with each other and ruin each other's houses?" "I don't know."

Yesterday COL Lentsov, Major Bushyhead, and I went to a brigade commanders' conference at TAB. The conference began at 1000 and ended at about 1530 with several short breaks. Lentsov was pretty disgusted at all the gum-beating. He found it amusing that at one point it was emphasized that affairs would not be tolerated, but at another point later there was calm discussion of medical evacuation of pregnant soldiers.

Today COL Lentsov and I are flying to a JMC meeting near Brcko, in COL Fontenot's AOR.

A couple of evenings ago at TAB a Russian soldier allegedly was groping an American female soldier, and when he wouldn't stop, she kneed him. Now he is being sent back to Russia in disgrace on the first available plane.

The Russians in Bosnia are a lot more cut off than we are. American planes land at TAB every day when weather permits, but only two planes a month are scheduled into TAB from Russia.

Sun, 10 Mar 96 1000

The JMC COL Lentsov and I attended Thursday included the largest number of high-ranking Bosnian Serbian, Muslim, and Croatian military officials assembled so far at a JMC. Most of it had to do with carrying out the military provisions of the Dayton Agreement for the period D+90 through D+120 (D-day having been 14 Dec 95).

Compliance with the military provisions of the Agreement seems to be going well, with the exception of mine-clearing, where it is just not physically possible for the FWPs to comply, that is, to clear as many as 4000 minefields in a matter of weeks in bad weather.

Mon, 11 Mar 96 0800

COL Lentsov thinks 90% of the military mission has been accomplished. The hard and problematical part is getting the civilian side going: police, local administrations, freedom of movement (FOM) for civilians and their resettlement, and restoration of the economy. That's why he has been working so hard to get the civilians on both sides to cooperating.

The Russians wish the Americans at Ugljevik would show up more at the Russian chow hall. Chief of Staff LTC Soloviev has escorted me to lunch personally twice, apparently on orders from COL Lentsov. Yesterday I went on my own accord and my presence was duly noted. It's a matter of self-image for the Russians. Their soup is usually pretty good, but the main course is sometimes pretty bad unless you like buckwheat, which I guess some people actually do. I joked to one of our people there yesterday that God is getting me for being a Russophile. [Not that MREs are anything to write home about and later, when we did start getting two hot meals a day across the river, for the most part it ran from fair to terrible.]

Fri, 15 Mar 96 0930

Major Tom Wilhelm thinks problems are arising with the Russians.

He and other Americans stationed at the RUS BDE have been accompanying Russian patrols and have been uncovering violations of the Dayton Agreement to which the Russians either react weakly or not at all. In particular, they have found armed Serbian soldiers in the ZOS, from which all armed personnel from the FWPs were to have been removed by D+30 (today is D+85).

Tom insists that he works for COL Lentsov and that he has not been snitching to HQ 1 AD, but the Russians probably do not believe him. Their response, according to Tom, has been to abruptly exclude Americans from their patrols.

1830

NATO Secretary General Javier Solana accompanied by GEN Joulwan and GEN Nash visited HQ RUS BDE this afternoon. COL Fontenot was also here.

COL Fontenot thinks he and COL Lentsov will be the last ones out of Bosnia, crossing the bridge across the Sava River back to back covering each other.

A civilian intruder shot at and wounded an American soldier somewhere in 2 BDE's sector about 0200 today. The soldier's partner fired 24 shots at the intruder, but failed to hit him and he got away.

Sun, 17 Mar 96 1130

Some of the small things in life:

I keep forgetting to ask for a second soap dish from home. Sooner or later I am going to lose the one I have [I never did] and if I don't have a replacement, that will be a major inconvenience.

Wet wipes are a major convenience, especially the kind that come in a canister so you can pull one at a time out the top. My normal rate of usage is one a day.

Chief of Staff COL Brown is expected out here today at a time that conflicts with my weekly shower.

We now have a contract barber who comes once a week. [That lasted about two weeks.] The Army pays for the haircuts. [The Army soon refused to do so and the fellows decided they'd rather cut each other's hair or even their own rather than pay.] Today the barber is set up in the presently empty room to the right as you come into my room from the hallway [through the door that says "Ne diraj lava dok spava" [neh] [dee-rai] [lah-vah] [dohk] [spah-vah] ("rai" as in "rye") (Don't touch a sleeping lion)]. I swept up my area this morning in anticipation of Chief Brown's visit, but in the last hour or so at least ten people have tracked through there in muddy boots. My broom is a whisk broom I had specially sent from Germany. The floor is made of some kind of fiber which never surrenders all of its dust.

Lots of things are free here: my room, my meals, transportation, the *Stars and Stripes*, my clothing (in principle), and probably some other things I haven't thought of.

Speaking of the *Stars and Stripes*, yesterday there was nearly a deluge of them—three issues, none more than ten days old.

Mon, 18 Mar 96 0900

Major Wilhelm says the problems with the Russians were the result of misunderstandings. Tom had substituted one American for another on one or more patrols without telling the Russians beforehand. In the American Army the expectation is that any officer of a given rank and general professional profile can substitute at any time for any other officer of the same rank and professional profile, while in the Russian army the system is much more personalized, more oriented toward individual personalities. And Tom had simply not been aware of that. And there were some other complications. Anyway, it all seems to have been smoothed over.

HQ 1 AD Chief of Staff Brown had a fine visit yesterday. [It's a good thing General Order No. 1 has an escape clause.]

Tues, 19 Mar 96 1100

We had a flap yesterday that seems to be ancient history today, maybe because today there's a new flap.

Day before yesterday the Bosnian Serbs began moving a column of heavy artillery pieces out of the British sector, way to the northwest of here, eastward across the northern part of 1 BDE's sector, and into the Russian sector toward Bijeljina with indications it would then move south through 2 BDE's sector and on into the French sector (which includes Sarajevo). The thing is that none of the FWPs are supposed to do that sort of thing without notifying IFOR a week in advance of just what is being moved where and certainly neither COL Fontenot at 1 BDE nor COL Lentsov at RUS BDE knew anything about it.

Evidently the Serbs got their artillery out of the British sector unobserved and were well into 1 BDE territory when we caught them. Then, rightly or wrongly, 1 BDE told them they could proceed on to Bijeljina. Now GEN Nash orders the Russians to bust their butts over to Bijeljina and put the artillery convoy under arrest until things could be sorted out. In other words, the Americans have been the nice guy cops and now the Russians are going to have to play the tough guy cop role, something they really don't like to do. Then, to make matters worse, the Serbs in Bijeljina show the Russian in charge, COL Breslavsky (see *Army Times*, 18

Mar 96, p.8), a document indicating that the Serbs had in fact complied with the notification requirement.

About 1900 yesterday COL Breslavsky burst into our office in a rage, just certain that the Americans had deliberately set the Russians up to be the fall guys.

The truth is much less dramatic.

In the first place, when the Brits failed to stop the Serbian artillery convoy, the American 1 BDE probably should have done so, and there are indications that there has been some buttock mastication on that account. But most important, nobody anywhere in IFOR seems to have received the notification, the probable reason being that the Bosnian Serb General Staff never passed it on, even though notification had been prepared at corps level.

Once again there was a potential for hard feelings, but some quick footwork seems to have mended things.

Today's flap presumably will be tomorrow's story.

Wed, 20 Mar 96 1030

Major Jeff Stimson, a FAO from the Marshall Center, has been on patrol with the Russians and confirms that they are not reacting very vigorously to ZOS violations by either side, saying, in effect, "Hey, we have to live with these guys and we don't want any trouble." This is at pretty serious variance with GEN Nash's policy and with IFOR policy in general and with the Dayton Agreement.

The first question is where this alternative policy comes from: is it COL Lentsov's policy or is it from a higher level, presumably from Moscow? Putting together what Lentsov says with what he does, it is my guess that it is his policy, but that he has backing for it from Moscow.

The second question is what to do. What we have been doing so far amounts to pestering the Russians to do what we want them to do. I think that sooner or later, and maybe better sooner than later, GEN Nash is going to have to have a serious, one-on-one discussion of the issue with

COL Lentsov. [I can't imagine now why I thought that—some dogs are better, MUCH better, left sleeping.]

Thurs, 21 Mar 96 1130

Craig Whitney of the *New York Times* was here this morning.

Sat, 23 Mar 96 0830

Major Jeff Stimson, a FAO from the MC, had adventures yesterday.

He and a Russian colonel (COL Yevgeny Georgievich Shamilin) were traveling in a Russian Uazik, a Jeep-like vehicle, south of here in the ZOS in or near a Muslim-populated area that is to be turned over to the Serbs in the next few days when they came upon a busload of some kind of Serbian special police. These fellows were armed with automatic weapons and big knives and looked pretty mean. IFOR is supposed to confiscate any such arms found in the ZOS, but Jeff and COL Shamilin weren't sure that the two of them plus their driver would be able to pull that off, so they merely told the Serbs they'd have to get out of the ZOS, which they did. Jeff says that in retrospect it would have been better to hightail it down the road about half an hour and come back with a couple of our Bradley fighting vehicles and crews.

At another point local Muslims, mainly old women, were demonstrating against the land transfers. They were putting rocks and other objects on the road. Jeff says they were being pretty emphatic in their objections.

The Sarajevo Federation government, that is, the Muslim-Croat Federation, wants the flag of Bosnia and Herzegovina, which encompasses both the Muslim-Croat Federation and the Republika Srpska, to hang over administrative buildings in the areas being transferred, while the Serbs insist that only the flag of Republika Srpska hang.

COL Shamilin asked our political adviser Felix Vargas for his reading on it, and Vargas said that the Dayton Agreement says nothing about flags and so IFOR should stay out of that argument. "A lot of help you are," Shamilin says, because both the Muslims and the Serbs seem to expect him to be able to do something about it.

Mid-day Thursday HQ 1 AD Operations Officer LTC Ed Kane came for an overnight visit to Russian Brigade Chief of Staff LTC Aleksandr Vasilievich Soloviev. They had met in Bad Kreuznach in November, but this was Kane's first trip to Ugljevik. They had numerous and pretty extensive discussions on matters both personal and professional. Kane didn't bring up the issue of Russian leniency toward Dayton Agreement violations. With the possible exception of potential trouble there, everything went swell. Yesterday morning we went out through Priboj and just the other side of Lopare, where we called in a practice air strike. The two planes that came were French and flew in from Italy, so we had an instance of French-Italian-American-Russian cooperation.

Our Air Force liaison guy, a LTC, told me that one of the reasons why things are often so hard in the Army is because they love their misery and squalor. For example, that this mission began just before Christmas rather than after gives them bragging rights. And that the hell they go through in Ranger training is not for the sake of the training, but of the hell.

I think the AF LTC may well be right. It's just striking, for example, how much grubbier the American Army is than the Russian Army, or at least their Airborne. The seats in Russian Uaziks are normal cushioned seats; the seats in Humvees are about an inch thick [actually, more like two inches] and feel pretty much like plywood wrapped in canvas. The Russians wash their Uaziks regularly; our Humvees out here are never washed. Etc, etc.

Sun, 24 Mar 96 0830

Things were less turbulent in the area being turned over to the Serbs yesterday, but not entirely quiet. Our guys think that if the Russians had gotten in there several weeks ago, made sure all weapons had been removed, and explained to the locals what was happening, things would have been quieter, as they have been in the AOTs (Areas of Transfer) in our 1st and 2nd Brigade sectors. But, albeit belatedly, the Russians do seem to be coping with the situation.

How at Dayton they ever managed to agree to turn Muslim villages over to the Serbs, I'll never understand. No matter what promises are made now, I can't imagine that the Serbs have any intention of letting these people live there in peace [later events were to bear this out].

One thing COL Lentsov did yesterday to quiet things down was to put up a big show of force—he ran a bunch of armored personnel carriers up and down the road a few times.

GEN Nash wants to see COL Lentsov at TAB this afternoon to talk about the situation.

Wed, 27 Mar 96 0745

The Muslims filed a flurry of complaints against the Russians right after the Russians arrived, and now there has been another flurry of them. Most of them are specious or based on a twisting of facts. But they have to be replied to, both to the Muslims and to British GEN Walker, Commander of the Allied Rapid Reaction Corps. The meeting with GEN Nash and his staff Sunday afternoon was about that.

GEN Nash says he thinks the Muslims are trying to drive a wedge between the Russians and the Americans. Both GEN Nash and COL Lentsov say that will not happen.

Monday COL Lentsov, Major Bushyhead, and I went to TAB to meet Hillary and Chelsea Clinton. I got to interpret a few sentences for them as they went down the line of brigade commanders. [Chelsea reminded me awfully strongly of Nika.]

Major Tom Wilhelm left Ugljevik Sunday. After a few days at TAB and in Germany he will return to his family in Florida, after which he and his family are to go to Dushanbe [doo-shahn-BEH], Tadjikistan, where he is to be stationed at the American Embassy. A year from now he will make LTC. Tom is a West Point graduate. [Tom made a real strong positive impression on me even without a thick, long black mustache.]

Yesterday we went back to TAB to a routine brigade commanders' conference and also for a meeting between COL Lentsov and GEN Cherrie to talk more about the Muslim complaints. [The plan had been to tell COL Lentsov that he had God-damned better kick some ass and get his brigade in shape, but I was so appalled to hear that that I suggested to Major Bushyhead that he advise Division not to do that. Major Bushyhead readily agreed.] [Thus] Major Bushyhead and I had advised that Cherrie trod very lightly on the issue of soldier discipline, and Cherrie started in real easy, starting with problems the Americans have experienced. After about five minutes of that, Lentsov interrupted and said Cherrie should skip the diplomacy and get to the point. Cherrie, looking much relieved, did so and I think they pretty much got to the truth. There have been instances of indiscipline, and Lentsov has already sent thirty soldiers back to Russia on that account. For example, a warrant officer got drunk publicly last week and he was out of the Army by the time his plane touched ground in Moscow. Had to buy his own ticket, too. And Lentsov doesn't doubt locals have been selling booze to Russian soldiers. But again the Muslims are hyping and twisting most of it.

That's a shame, because I believe the Russians are truly being evenhanded in their treatment of the Muslims and Serbs. On Sunday COL Lentsov made an impassioned plea on behalf of the Muslims in his area who are being turned over arbitrarily to the Serbs.

This is three Muslim villages which have been Muslim for centuries and where there were no great perturbations during the war. That is, a turnover to the Serbs is totally unjustified. And no matter what the Serbs promise now, the truth is that after the turnover the Serbs will make their lives so miserable that they will leave.

Thurs, 28 Mar 96 0830

The weather has been spring-like the past week or so and a lot of spring plowing has been going on. It rained all day yesterday. During the night it turned sharply colder and this morning we have an inch or so of wet snow with more coming down, although lightly.

Yesterday morning Major Bushyhead and I attended a meeting in Tuzla between COL Lentsov and the Commander of the 25th Division of the Army of BiH (Bosnia and Herzegovina). The meeting went well.

We spent the afternoon at TAB.

First we spent about 20 minutes with GEN Nash going over COL Lentsov's version of the incident of the arrest by the Serbians of the Muslim mayor of Teocak [TEH-o-chahk] (the "o" in Teocak comes from a historical "l" just as it does in every word in Serbo-Croatian in which an "o" follows a vowel and precedes a consonant or is the last sound/letter in the word).

On 22 March COL Lentsov had assured all and sundry, including the mayor of Teocak, that civilians traveling in civilian vehicles without weapons would not be hindered in their travels across the ZOS.

On 23 March the Mayor of Teocak drove into Priboj, which is in the ZOS on the Serbian side. He was made to accompany Serbian police to Lopare, where he was taken to the Chief of Police and treated to coffee and a bottle of beer.

Then he was tested for alcohol and taken to the Bijeljina jail along with three others who had been in the car.

That evening he was tried for and convicted of DWI and disturbing the peace, for each of which he was given five days' arrest. On the 26th he was accused of having hidden an explosive device under the driver's seat of his car.

On the 25th, I think it was, someone from the Muslim side told the Russians about the arrest. The Russians got right on it and on the 26th, along with a representative of the IPTF (International Police Task Force), were allowed to talk to the Mayor of Teocak in the Bijeljina jail. The mayor said they were not being maltreated and that aside from the beer, several hours earlier he had drunk 100 grams of brandy. None of which justifies the Serbs, but does put a shading on it.

Anyway, the point that interests Nash is that the Russians have acted promptly and vigorously in defense of a Muslim.

At 1400 GEN Delic, Commander of the ABiH 2nd Corps, and the commander of the 28th ABiH Division were shown in. The meeting with them went on for two hours. Lentsov went through the matter again. And other business was covered. Afterwards GEN Nash told Lentsov that he had played it splendidly. One of the things Nash suggested Lentsov could do is to hold a press conference to cast unfavorable light on the Serbs if they don't release the Mayor of Teocak pretty soon.

1345

But as of this writing, the Mayor of Teocak is still being held by the Serbs.

An OSCE (Organization of Security and Cooperation in Europe) group was just here talking to COL Lentsov. They are supposed to handle the civilian side of the Dayton Agreement.

An NBC radio correspondent had a recording of a Russian officer talking to Muslims in one of the areas to be turned over to the Serbs. Somehow the Muslims got the idea the Russians were telling them (at 1100) that they had to abandon all and leave by 1500, when the Serbs would come. Although the Russians denied having done any such thing (they said the Russian officer had told the locals that negotiations were taking place in Sarajevo, the results of which would become known at 1500), some of our people weren't sure. When the correspondent, a young woman, asked Major Bushyhead at TAB yesterday whether his interpreter would translate the tape for her, he said sure. So yesterday early in the evening she drove all the way out here alone. But someone had alerted HQ 1 AD Chief of Staff COL Brown, who said nothin' doin'. God forbid an American should uncover something bad the Russians had done. Major Bushyhead and a couple of FAOs listened to the tape and it completely vindicated the Russians. I hope (and assume) the reporter made her way back to Tuzla safely.

Tuesday morning we were due at TAB at 0930 to see GEN Cherrie and we were to travel with COL Lentsov in Lentsov's Uazik. Lentsov told Bushyhead twice that we would leave at 0800 on the dot. At about 0740 John ambled across the Elbe (on the new bridge) for breakfast with our people. At 0757 Viktor, COL Lentsov's adjutant, popped his head into our office door and said, "Let's go!" I called quick across the river and then ran out and got in the Uazik. At 0800, just as Major Bushyhead was running toward the parking lot, Lentsov said, "Go!" and off we went in a cloud of dust, but without Bushyhead, even though I did utter a peep in his behalf. He was in luck, though, as it turned out a second Russian Uazik departed for TAB about 20 minutes later, so hardly anyone was the wiser and I'm pretty sure Bushyhead will never cut it so close with Lentsov again.

Sat, 30 Mar 96 0830

Our trip to TAB yesterday was to meet with representatives from OSCE who are to organize the elections which are supposed to take place throughout Bosnia and

70

Herzegovina in September. The head of the group was a Russian, Vladimir Ivanov, who speaks excellent English. Their prognosis for the successful holding of elections was a gloomy one, for a whole number of reasons.

1145

This morning GEN Nash, COL Lentsov, Major Bushyhead, and I flew out and a number of other Americans and Russians and also the press drove out to a site northeast of Brcko to inspect a declared site where the Serbs are concentrating and storing anti-aircraft and other weapons. GEN Nash was not impressed with the quality and quantity of the equipment we were shown and wonders whether they aren't hiding things from us. COL Lentsov thinks that by making the Serbs concentrate and account for what they have we are helping them accomplish internal reorganization, which will be of advantage to them when they redeploy right after IFOR leaves (presumably in December).

Mon, 1 Apr 96 1000

SecDef Perry was supposed to visit us yesterday, but bad weather prevented flying, so GEN Sigutkin with his interpreter and COL Lentsov, Major Bushyhead, and I drove in to TAB, where Sigutkin and Lentsov briefed the SecDef. Sigutkin's interpreter, CPT Gennadii Kamenev, did most of the interpreting.

The main thrust of what Sigutkin, Lentsov, and the SecDef had to say was how well the Russians and Americans are working together. Which in fact is true.

Thurs, 4 Apr 96 0815

The sensation of the day, of course, is the crash of Secretary of Commerce Brown's plane with not only his loss, but that, as I understand it, of a lot of people who could have helped Bosnia financially.

The mayor of Teocak has been released; I'm not sure about the other three who were with him.

Fri, 5 Apr 96 0815

A week or so ago a Serbian woman was killed by a mine near one of the Russian checkpoints. Yesterday three Polish soldiers were severely injured by a mine; two lost their right legs and the third may have lost an eye.

TAB Flight Line
Mon, 8 Apr 96 0930

I'm not supposed to be here.

A couple of months ago some purple spots appeared on several of my toes on both feet. My feet had gotten pretty cold several times and sometimes my toes hurt pretty badly when they're cold. But I didn't do anything about it except tell Rosemary by phone. She suggested I take a picture and send her.

So Friday evening I asked Major Bushyhead to take a close-up picture of my toes. This brought the matter to his attention, and Saturday morning he had me go to our medic, who in turn referred me to the 212th MASH at Camp Bedrock south of TAB.

I was at the 212th by 1700 or so Saturday. Three doctors examined me. None of them had seen anything quite like it before. They did establish that I have poor circulation to the extremities, especially the lower ones, but I knew that anyway. There are two possibilities: damage due to cold or embolisms. They were reluctant to diagnose cold injury for two reasons: 1st, they might be wrong and it might be something far more serious, and 2nd, there weren't supposed to be any cold injuries because that would be an indication of command failure at some level. They ran all the tests they could, but couldn't find anything that might cause embolisms. So no diagnosis here.

The next step is the Army hospital at Landstuhl, Germany. In the next hour or so I am to board a C-130 bound for Ramstein AB. By 1400 today I should be at the hospital. Rosemary is going to meet me there (it is exactly four months today since I left Garmisch). My guess and hope is that the diagnosis will be not very severe cold injury and that I will be back in Bosnia by the end of the week.

I was stupid, of course, not to go to the medics when the spots first appeared. But I didn't think I had much of a problem and I don't like to complain. And this will raise Cain with my hero image.

About noon yesterday word came in to the 212th MASH that a Russian soldier had stepped on a mine and lost a leg. A medevac helicopter was on the way. The 212th was ready to receive the soldier, and I volunteered my services as interpreter, but the Russians decided to take the soldier to their facility at Ugljevik. I learned later in the day that the amputation was below the knee.

Ramstein AB, Germany
Mon, 15 Apr 96 0930

The Russian soldier lost both feet and was returned to Russia Thursday, according to yesterday's *Stars and Stripes*.

Rosemary and Nika arrived at the Landstuhl hospital before I did. I was immediately examined by Dr. (Major) Andrew Scanameo and also by a Dr. Richie, dermatologist. They had never seen anything quite like what I have, either. Lots of tests were run, in particular the Echo test to check for possible heart problems, and a biopsy was done. By Thursday afternoon it was 95% certain it was a cold injury, so Rosemary and Nika left early Friday morning, and by Friday afternoon it was 100%.

I was never admitted as an in-patient to the Landstuhl hospital. Instead we all stayed at the American guest house right next to the hospital, at very modest cost, I might add.

So we had several pretty nice days, hitting the bookstores and PX pretty heavily, among other things. I was able to luxuriate in unlimited hot water showers, which was especially nice. Everyone, and first of all Dr. Scanameo, was very good to us.

The drive for Rosemary was six hours each way from Garmisch.

Saturday morning I got up at 0200 and was at the Ramstein AB passenger terminal by 0330. There were several C-130 flights to TAB that day, but I didn't make any of them because my civilian ID card had expired in February. That I had several other valid ID cards and also valid TDY orders didn't cut any ice, and nobody could be mobilized to help me, so here I am Monday morning. Very frustrating.

I had made noises about the expired ID in February, but at best it was going to be a hassle to renew it in Bosnia, so I decided to let it go until June, since I didn't seem to need it in Bosnia, anyway. And I mistakenly assumed I could go back to Bosnia on my IFOR and other IDs and my TDY orders. Otherwise I would have made the effort and gotten the ID renewed last week.

So I got another 48 hours of hot water showers—I stayed at the guest house here, where again they were very good to me, especially the manager, whose name I didn't get, but he looks like a younger Elia Kazan. [Note of 31 May 2004: I confused Elia Kazan with someone else.]

Barring unforeseen problems I should be back at TAB by 1800 today and in Ugljevik by tomorrow evening.

TAB
Wed, 17 Apr 96 1100

Monday afternoon the airport bus was rolling up to our C-130's hardstand just as the C-130 started taxiing out. For whatever reason the C-130's crew had decided to leave without taking any passengers. That left about 15 of us

74

stranded, including a number of Air Force people. No local billets were available, so I joined the AF people and spent the night at an expensive hotel in Kaiserslautern.

It wasn't clear that we would be able to leave yesterday, either, but a special flight was laid on to take passengers only, all told about 40 of us, perhaps in part at least because the AF people had successfully raised a fuss. We left Ramstein about 1630 and arrived at TAB about 1900.

It was bright and clear in Germany yesterday; when we arrived here it was raining hard.

I probably won't get back to Ugljevik until tomorrow.

They say my services have been missed at the Russian Brigade, GEN Nash in particular wanting to know when I'll be back and Chief of Staff Soloviev saying everything has gone to hell since I've been gone. At any rate GEN Nash stepped into the Russian Liaison Office this morning, slapped me on the back, asked how my feet were, and welcomed me back.

COL Ashikhmin has been replaced by a COL Zamotayev. Board sidewalks have been set up down TAB's main drag.

I'm being put up at visiting VIP quarters, which are luxurious by U.S. Army standards in Bosnia and not bad by any standards. There's even a sink with hot and cold water in my room.

Ugljevik Power Station, HQ RUS BDE
Fri, 19 Apr 96 0900

I finally got back to Ugljevik yesterday, after 12 days' absence.

A Nordic/Polish brigade vehicle hit a mine Wed, killing a Danish and a Lithuanian soldier and wounding two Danish soldiers. The entire Lithuanian contingent in Bosnia consists of one platoon (22 soldiers), so proportionately it is a very heavy loss for them.

75

Yesterday afternoon one of the tracks on a Swedish APC came apart as they were crossing a bridge, causing the APC to swerve and drop off the bridge. Two Swedish soldiers were killed.

COL GEN Shevtsov, GEN Joulwan's deputy at SHAPE for the Russian Brigade, began a 3-day visit to the RUS BDE yesterday.

One of the first things he did was to raise hell about the state of their battery chargers for communications. What started that was when he was unable to communicate with anyone from the checkpoint in the mountain pass on Route Georgia. As Major Bushyhead puts it, he ripped their lips off.

Mon, 22 Apr 96 0845

Friday afternoon there was a meeting here of senior VRS (Vojska [VOY-skah] Republike Srpske—Army of the Republika Srpska), and ABiH military leaders with GENs Nash and Shevtsov. Shevtsov chaired it. The main topic was how the VRS and ABiH military assess the situation as of D+120, which was Fri, 19 Apr 96. All agreed that the military provisions of the Dayton Agreement are being carried out for the most part, but that the civilian side is lagging badly.

A major topic was the wish of Muslim refugees in Celic to visit their former homes and also cemeteries across the line in Koraj [koh-rai]. The Russians are urging the Muslims to keep the numbers down and avoid publicity. The Muslims want to send about 2500 people across the line at one time, which is sure to cause trouble.

After the meeting we all went to the Commander's Field Mess for a good meal and where the vodka flowed. It turned out that some of the VRS and ABiH military knew each other from their service together in the JNA (Yugoslav National Army). Everyone was very friendly, all difficult to reconcile with the bloody war they waged against each other (in reference to which see especially David Rieff's *Slaughterhouse: Bosnia and the Failure of the West*, New York: Simon & Schuster, 1996 [and Laura Silber and Allan Little's *The Death of Yugoslavia*, London: Penguin Books, 2nd edition, 1996]).

GEN Shevtsov returned to SHAPE Saturday.

Major Bushyhead is going on his two-week R&R leave today. His stand-in is Major John Cecil, who has replaced Rich Choppa (traded places, actually, as Choppa is now at TAB).

I've been talking to Jeff Stimson and John Cecil about how they evaluate the Russians. They wouldn't go so far as to call them Nicaraguans with nuclear bombs, like Bushyhead does, but they are pretty critical. More about that later.

Spring seems to have come: it's warm and sunny, supposed to be in the 70's today (20+C).

1930

The big deal for the next few days is going to be keeping the Muslim march on Koraj from getting out of hand. COL Lentsov is urging Division to help damp it down.

Tues, 23 Apr 96 1415

It was just reported that the Serb police are committing some kind of outrage in the southern part of the Russian sector near Zvornik. I was the one who brought it to the attention of the Russians here at Brigade HQ.

Wed, 24 Apr 96 0900

The information on yesterday's incident is incomplete and to some extent contradictory.

LTC Dementiev, CDR of the Russian 1st Battalion at Priboj, told me that it was Muslims shooting stray dogs and furthermore that the Muslims had informed them ahead of time about it. But the IPTF seemed to believe that the Serbian police were taking actions against Muslims that included shooting and burning. The Russians sent a ground patrol to investigate and 1 AD sent helicopters.

HQ 1 AD is unhappy with the reports the Russians sent, finding them incomplete and contradictory. Major Cecil believes that the RUS BDE staff does bad work because their Chief of Staff is organizationally weak and doesn't get the support and guidance he needs from the COMBRIG (COL Lentsov). Whether or not this is true or typical of staff work in the Russian Army is a different question. Cecil says that one occasionally runs across the same problem at brigade and battalion HQ in the American Army. But the implication is that it happens less often with us than with the Russians.

1130
Twice today we have pulled the rug out from under the Russians.

A visit by GEN O'Neal to the RUS BDE to discuss matters of supply has been planned for some time. It was supposed to have taken place today, and apparently the Russians had gone to considerable effort to prepare for it. This morning we announced that the visit is cancelled.

A helicopter recon flight with the Russians was supposed to take place today, too, but we cancelled the helicopter.

Wed, 24 Apr 96 1330

A couple of Serbs clearing mines were injured when one exploded just a little bit ago. The Russians called for and then cancelled medevac.

Mon, 29 Apr 96 1030

Most of the news these days has to do with Muslim attempts to visit graveyards and former homes now on the

Serbian side of the IEBL (Inter-Entity Boundary Line). In the Russian sector that's the village Dugi Dio (in Russian that would probably be "Dolgij Del") in the south, near Sapna (mentioned in the *Stars and Stripes* Sun, 28 Apr 96) and Celic-Koraj. So far there has been no major trouble, but the potential may be there. Keeping a watch on the situation is keeping us pretty busy. Sometimes it seems like all Major Cecil has to do is leave the office and the phone will start ringing about every other minute. Representatives from the ECMM (European Commission of Military Monitors) have been coming by pretty regularly, too. The Russians call them "ice-cream guys" (morozhenshchiki [mah-ROH-zhin-shchee-kee]) because they dress in white. LTC Jack Humphries, XO (Executive Officer, i.e. Chief of Staff) at 2nd BDE, and LTC Marvin Englert, XO at 1st BDE, were guests of RUS BDE Chief of Staff Soloviev yesterday from about 1400 to 1900. I was interpreter throughout. Mainly it was a get-acquainted and get-out-of-the-office session, and I think the three of them genuinely enjoyed each other's company. Unlike some sessions involving COL Lentsov, the amount of vodka poured for each toast was held to about one American shot. But there were quite a few toasts. The soldiers accompanying the XOs played volleyball, etc, with their Russian counterparts. Soloviev really wants to know whether the American soldiers truly had a good time here while they were with Russian soldiers. I expect they did.

CPT Vlad Petnicki, GEN Nash's Serbo-Croatian interpreter, got a write-up in Saturday's *Stars and Stripes*. I have worked with Petnicki several times and had a pretty long talk with him recently. One thing not mentioned in the article is that his name is of Slovak origin, so Serbs, Croats, and Muslims cannot immediately determine his ethnicity. Anyway, Petnicki's main claim to fame is that his father, who is still living, was Tito's interpreter for half a dozen languages.

We have two new Serbo-Croatian interpreters, one a Muslim who says he is not at all interested in Islam and that the only thing Serbs can have against him is his last name.

79

The other is a Serb from Serbia proper (rather than from Bosnia). We've put them in the same room and expect no problems. The reason we hired them is that the Russians have only one Serbo-Croatian speaker in their brigade and have only hired one local, which is not nearly enough. Since Americans go out on Russian patrols, the new interpreters work ostensibly for us, but in fact largely for the Russians.

I asked the Russians' interpreter recently whether being hired by the Russians was a stroke of good luck for him, and a Russian officer sitting next to him said it would be if they paid him, but so far they haven't. It's going to be too bad if it turns out the ones we have hired are in a far better position. I understand we are paying them DM 1000 a month (about $700). [Note inserted 8 May 96: the Russians' interpreter is getting DM 500 a month.]

COL Lentsov promised to take Major Cecil with him to Lopare and Celic today, but then ran off and left him. That happens a lot to Major Bushyhead, too. [Note inserted 8 May 96: Lentsov later dropped by and apologized, saying he had simply forgotten.]

1700

A small cafe out by the parking lot has opened with chairs and tables set up in front of it, but under a roof. A can of Coca-Cola costs DM 1.50 or $1. After the XOs left yesterday I sat there for an hour or so with three Russian captains. One of them, not having his own apartment, pays $100 out of his salary of $200 a month to rent an apartment plus $20 a month for parking his car in a closed enclosure. Doesn't leave much to live on.

Theoretically we can take hot showers in our building. First you check that there's pressure, then screw in a fuse on a panel, and in about half an hour the water will be hot. The practical problem is that at least today the pressure through the hot water pipe was about enough to get yourself wet, not more. Fortunately, the pressure through the cold water pipe was better and the ambient air temperature was warm enough in the middle of the day to make a cold shower bearable.

1830

Major Cecil finds the Russians very frustrating.

I've been eating breakfast with the Americans lately, but I can barely force myself to eat greasy scrambled eggs and greasy potato whatever-it-is. For a time I found the Russian dining hall fairly good, but lately I've found it hard to get their stuff down, too. Basically since I came back from Landstuhl.

Yesterday afternoon I left a Walkman and my camera on my desk at work. When I came back at 1900 the $50 Walkman was gone, but the $200 camera was still there. Shouldn't have left them out, of course. Several weeks ago Major Bushyhead caught the soldier detailed to guard our building in his room. When the soldier's things were searched, Major Bushyhead's Walkman, which had been missing for some time, was found plus some other things.

LTC Soloviev told me yesterday he thinks Major Cecil is too much of an American (excessively American in character). [He apparently meant insufficiently laid back.]

Tues, 30 Apr 96 1215

The event of the day is the march of the Muslims from Celic to Koraj. The agreement seems to have been that three busloads of Muslims would cross a bridge and travel to Koraj. One version is that the buses would go one at a time, each waiting until the preceding one had returned with its passengers. The three buses, loaded with passengers aged 50 and up, a list of which has been turned over to the Serbs, are at the bridge. Crowds have collected on both sides with sticks and stones and bad words. The buses aren't moving. The Russians are there. The IPTF came and left. International reporters are there (read all about it in tomorrow's *Stars and Stripes*). We have had helicopters overhead.

Carl Bildt, former Prime Minister of Sweden and currently United Nations High Commissioner for Refugees, arrived here by helicopter at 1215 and is on the way to meet with the local authorities in Bijeljina, after which he is to return here for lunch and a briefing with the Russians. Both the American and Russian military believe these marches are a Muslim provocation and political maneuver and are trying not to get dragged into maintaining civil order, that is, carrying out police functions. Lentsov says it is fine by him if they want to pound each other's mugs, just so there are no weapons, which he is mandated to confiscate. He has authority to search for weapons.

GEN Nash and COL Lentsov are in frequent contact. And in general the phone is in constant use.

The "ice cream guys" were here most of the morning.

1630

Carl Bildt's helicopter just lifted off to return him to Sarajevo. He had arrived back from Bijeljina at 1430, was briefed by COL Lentsov, and then dined at the Russian dining hall. He brought several bottles of Swedish whiskey with him, of which he was not about to partake in the Russian fashion.

Thurs, 2 May 96 0915

Yesterday was May Day and for the most part RUS BDE stood down.

GEN Sigutkin was replaced on 25 Apr by GEN Viktor Andreyevich Sorokin. So far we don't have much of a feel for GEN Sorokin. GEN Shevtsov when he was here wrote a letter giving directions as to how orders and dispositions to the RUS BDE from HQ 1 AD are to be handled and as to the functions of the Vukosavci group (GEN Sorokin's group). GEN Nash is concerned about this and tried most of the day yesterday to get COL Lentsov on the phone to talk about it. But GEN Nash did not mention it during this morning's telephone conference.

Warm spring weather does wonders for one's mood.

Fri, 3 May 96 1515

Chief of Staff COL Brown came out today. Strictly a routine visit.

Mon, 6 May 96 0750

Medevac in progress. A Russian soldier with a bullet wound to the chest is being brought here from Priboj, from where he will be taken by helicopter to the 212th MASH at Bed Rock. Our initial notice was at 0739. As of 0758 the wounded man was at the Medical Point [Medpunkt] here.

0815
Helicopter turned back due to bad weather. Two men injured in an accident. One has two bullet wounds to the chest, the other a bullet wound to the shoulder. The weather here is OK, but the mountain pass may be socked in.

0822
The helicopter is here.

0858
Two medevac helicopters are here.

0925
Helicopter lift-off.

0929
Second helicopter lifts off.

0940

Major Cecil just came in to say that one of the soldiers died, time given as 0903. The other soldier is being stabilized and may or may not be medevaced subsequently.

1100

The mood around RUS BDE HQ is real grim.

Tues, 7 May 96 0700

The young man who was killed was 19 and had been in the Army six months. As it happens, a Russian plane is due in today and will transport back to Russia the body and also under escort the "criminal," as Chief of Staff Soloviev put it, whose fault it was. So a momentary act of carelessness with a dangerous weapon has cut off one young life and severely blighted another, plus the hurt to those closest to both of them. The wounded man, also, it turns out, with a chest wound, may or may not be put on the plane, depending on his condition. I was told he was operated on for seven hours yesterday.

Wed, 8 May 96 0745

The Russian soldiers had been issued live ammunition for an exercise, but weapons were not supposed to have been loaded yet. Several of them were joking around in their barracks. One of them aimed his rifle at another and pulled the trigger. Two shots were fired in rapid succession (full automatic, presumably). One soldier received massive injuries to the chest area, the other lesser injuries to the stomach with the liver taking a nick. The very worst sort of safety violation: aiming an unloaded weapon at someone— only it wasn't unloaded. COL Lentsov says the perpetrator will probably get four or five years jail time, maybe more.

I went to TAB yesterday with COL Lentsov. The first order of business was to be to meet with GEN Nash and

GEN Malkic, the commander of the ABiH 28th Division. Apparently they have more complaints against the Russians. The ABiH commander went to what used to be the main gate to TAB, which is now closed to vehicle traffic, and on being told he would have to drive around to the other gate got mad and left. He may have been glad of an excuse not to bring up the complaints, which in the past have not been well founded.

One way or another four or five Russian generals were at the flight line. I had seen GEN Staskov at Ugljevik the day before, GEN Sorokin was there, and I guess a general from Eastern Slavonia, because a Russian UN unit from there was leaving, or at least a large number of their personnel. And at some point Lentsov's first general's star was pinned on his shoulders. A little bit after that the Russian plane landed and GEN Lentsov met his wife Marina, who will be here until the next plane two weeks from now.

She had an adventure. No visa is required for Russians to come here, but a Russian customs official tried to scratch her off the passenger list for not having one (visas aren't Customs business, anyway, that's for the Border Guards). But for a fee of $600 he could fix it. Marina only had $130 on her, she gave him that, and was allowed on the plane.

While we were waiting for the Russian plane a C-130 pilot provided some entertainment. He was coming in parallel but to the right of the landing strip and high, but rather than going around for another try, he stood the C-130 first on its left wing and then on the right and then dived steeply. I wasn't sure he'd be able to pull out, and the Russians watching, mainly or all Airborne, after all, were clearly astonished.

GEN Nash inquired about my feet, gave me a little lecture on foot care, and said he'd make a soldier of me yet.

He also told me to find out when Staskov came and to make sure he got on the Russian plane and left.

GEN Nash asked when Major Bushyhead was returning. I said, "Today," and he said, "Good."

85

Major Bushyhead arrived back at TAB yesterday afternoon from his R&R to the States and should be out here late today.

Sat, 11 May 96 1130

Thurs, 9 May 96, was the 51st Anniversary of Victory in the Great Patriotic War, as the Russians call their part of the Second World War. It is a much bigger deal for them than it is for us, and they put on a big celebration at Vukosavci, where their administrative support element is located. About 25 Americans were there as official guests, headed by GEN Nash, as well as an honor guard and our band.

As we were stepping up to the podium for GEN Nash's speech, he apologized for not getting a copy of it to me beforehand and afterwards he said, "Jim, you ain't worth a sack o' shit," which I guess has to be taken as high praise since in fact I didn't stumble too badly as he spoke.

After the dinner I talked some to Mr. Bogdanovic, mayor of Lopare, mainly through the Russian Serbo-Croatian interpreter, CPT Aleksei Bosykh (not to be confused with their Bosnian Serbian Serbo-Croatian interpreter). In talking to Serbs I sometimes wonder just who I am talking to. I'd like to think that Bogdanovic is all right. He wanted me to teach him how to appeal in English to the Americans to quit ruining his roads with their tanks and also for me to pass on his request to our people. They certainly do need help with their roads, and not just for the ones the Americans have been driving tanks and Bradleys over.

GEN Sorokin, head of the Vukosavci group, emphasized to me that he was a general not of Russia, but of the Soviet Union. He thinks the Americans have no business being in Bosnia, that it is not in our interests to be there, and that this is an area where Russians should be predominant. And echoing a line from Zhirinovsky's scandalous autobiography *The Last Lunge South*, he opined that Russian

86

soldiers should be washing their boots in the warm waters of the Indian Ocean. [He also said he knew that GEN Nash had had GEN Staskov kicked out. When some time later I told GEN Nash what Sorokin had said, he said it wasn't true, but he didn't mind if people thought it was.]

LT GEN Abrams, 5th Corps CG and therefore GEN Nash's superior, had stated beforehand that the Americans would be observing General Order No. 1, i.e. would partake of no alcohol. But he was to arrive some time after the dinner was well under way, so GEN Nash gave at least tacit permission for the Americans to participate in toasts. GEN Abrams when he arrived didn't make a fuss about it, but personally refused to partake. It's a serious matter, because when Russians say only Fascists won't drink toasts to Victory Day, they're not kidding.

The weather cooperated for the most part and the event was a big success as far as I could determine.

LTC Soloviev, Russian Brigade Chief of Staff, got pretty high. I came back to Ugljevik with him and CPT Aleksei Bosykh, the Russian Serbo-Croatian interpreter. On the way we stopped at a cafe for a beer and coffee and to talk some more. We were there for quite awhile, until well after dark, and I didn't know where we were, not realizing we were only a hundred feet or so from the Priboj intersection.

As we prepared to leave, I went to the WC. When I came out LTC Soloviev and Aleksei had disappeared, so I walked down to the Uazik and got in. A few minutes later Soloviev and Aleksei appeared again among the tables in front of the cafe talking to people there. Hearing Soloviev mention the Americans, I decided to rejoin him and Aleksei, who were talking to some young men at a table. I offered to take their picture, but they indicated I shouldn't. It became clear they didn't like Americans—how come we were their allies in WWI and WWII, but not now, why had we bombed them, why do we favor the Muslims, etc. One of them, who seemed to dominate, said he had fought in the war. Soloviev even in his condition realized this wasn't going well and told me to fade out, which I was glad to do. Some awful things happened during the war and at least some of them were done by people who like to do that sort of thing, I didn't know where we were, we didn't have any arms in evidence and Soloviev was in no condition to use his pistol even if he wanted, and I began to wonder what we might be getting ourselves in for. But Soloviev and Aleksei disengaged and we left peacefully. Plus it turned out we were in familiar territory, not more than a kilometer or so from part of the Russian garrison in Priboj, where shots would have been heard. But I was scared.

Yesterday GEN Lentsov, his wife, and I went to TAB, where the meeting with Muslim GEN Malkic scheduled for Tuesday finally took place. Mainly Malkic talked, all told about an hour and a half. CPT Petnicki translated into English and then I translated that into Russian for Lentsov, although he could understand some of what Malkic was saying without translation. Under pressure from GEN Nash, Malkic admitted progress is being made both on freedom of movement (FOM) and return of refugees [not much, I've got to say]. But much of what he said is true and troubling: fair and valid elections in September are nearly impossible and the war is likely to renew if IFOR leaves in December-January and is not replaced.

GEN Lentsov is probably leaving in July. LTC Soloviev will remain for the time being, at least.

Tues, 14 May 96 0730

Saturday we were visited by the editors of nine mostly well-known American newspapers, the *Atlanta Constitution*, etc. They had a press conference with GEN Lentsov and then were escorted by the Russian and American military to Bijeljina for dinner with and speeches by important Serbian civilians, starting with the Mayor of Bijeljina. What they got, then, is the official Serb line.

The main point of which is that they are willing to be good neighbors to the Muslims, but they don't want to live with them anymore. Most of the few Serbs who do try to return to their old homes on what is now Muslim territory have bad experiences and come back to Serbian territory, they say. They assert that the Turks (an ethnic slur when used in reference to Bosnian Muslims), unlike Orthodox Christians, have no tradition of visiting or keeping up graveyards, and so all this fuss about graveyard visits amounts to political manipulation (that may well be true). They need and hope for international economic aid, but don't expect to get very much.

It does seem to me that whatever nice words were written into the Dayton Agreement about FOM and the right of refugees to return to their homes, it is just not going to happen. The Serbs have largely achieved their main war aim—ethnic cleansing and separation—and they are not going to let very many Muslims back onto their territory, even if it costs them terribly in lost economic aid. I am not so sure, for that matter, that Serbs are welcome on Muslim-Croat Federation territory.

My guess is that eventually the international community will reconcile itself to this and will settle for achievement of a state of non-war and three separate countries in Bosnia, with the Croatian part probably eventually being incorporated into Croatia and the Serbian part (Republika Srpska) into Serbia-Montenegro.

That is to say, there is not going to be any coherent and effective Muslim-Croat Federation, either. The main problem with that is that it leaves the Muslims landlocked, which hinders arms deliveries to them, and leaves them an economic basket case.

Wed, 15 May 96 0900

A minor flap that came from the editors' meeting with Serb officials in Bijeljina is that we unintentionally stiffed the Serbs with the bill for the meal.

A bigger flap this week is the case of the "Zvornik Seven." Last week seven armed Muslims surrendered to American soldiers on Serbian territory, evidently because they were on the verge of being captured by the Serbs, to whom we turned them over anyway. They claim to have just come out of six months' hiding, but they are suspected of being some kind of Muslim hit squad, perhaps sent to fire on IFOR forces so that the Serbs would get the blame. They are also suspected of killing four Serbian wood-cutters last week.

Five of the "Zvornik Seven" are in the Bijeljina jail, where Major Bushyhead saw them on Monday. He says they didn't look like they had just come out of six months' hiding. On the other hand, it was clear that the Serbian police had been beating the living daylights out of them. And supposedly at least one has ratted on the rest.

0930

A shower container was set up across the river about a week ago, so we can shower just about any time we want to, providing we haven't run out of water, which has to be trucked in. And a couple of days ago we got a retransmitter for AFN radio on FM and also, via the same satellite, AFN TV, which is fed by cable to the mess hall tent. We have laundry service now, too. On the other hand, the Army refused to contract a barber for us.

The U.S. Army through a contractor pays Serbo-Croatian interpreters DM 1000 a month. Yesterday I was told that the Russians are paying their interpreter DM 350 a month (DM1000 = $675; DM350 = $236).

Fri, 17 May 96 0845

The Russians have lost another soldier. Yesterday evening a soldier was doing something with a field telephone and was electrocuted. Chief of Staff Soloviev was REAL grim this morning.

The American ambassador to Hungary, Donald Blinken, paid a brief visit to RUS BDE yesterday, accompanied by GENs Nash and Abrams.

GEN Nash will be back today to meet with Bosnian Serb GEN Gavric.

Wed, 22 May 96 0930

GEN Gavric had arranged for dinner after his meeting with GEN Nash. Both the meeting and the dinner took place at the Ugljevik Power Plant administration building, which is a fine modern building in contrast to the buildings occupied by the RUS BDE right next door.

The meeting and subsequent dinner went on and on and on. I got in on the latter part of the dinner, to which a Russian observer had also been invited. Then Gavric invited Nash to Bijeljina for ice cream, so we all piled into two Russian armored personnel carriers and a bunch of Humvees and off we went to Bijeljina. In Bijeljina we drove a considerable distance down narrow streets (Humvees and esp. APCs are very wide), ending up at a restaurant called the "Vladivostok," where we sat outside, as it was a very nice, warm day. The servings of ice cream were very generous.

After the ice cream visit GEN Nash and party were taken to a small airport just this side of Bijeljina, from where he and his party departed by helicopter.

That the afternoon with GEN Gavric went on so much longer than scheduled and was so conspicuously cordial is intriguing in light of reported differences of opinion within the Bosnian Serb leadership between the hardliners and the moderates.

I think Bijeljina and the area between Ugljevik and Bijeljina looks pretty good. It is obvious that the standard of living here was pretty good before the war.

Sat, 18 May GEN Lentsov had his driver and adjutant take Marina (Lentsov's wife) and me first to the Swedish PX at the Swedish base the other side of Tuzla and then to the PX at TAB.

Marina was mainly interested in some items of clothing for her husband and son and was careful with her money.

Lentsov's adjutant bought ten huge bottles of Smirnoff vodka plus a bunch of other stuff. Marina was appalled.

After a look through the American PX at TAB, where they didn't buy so much, we went to lunch at the dining hall, which was practically deserted since it was mid-afternoon. The salad bar especially impressed Marina; she couldn't seem to get over it. We sat down at a table where an American Army captain was sitting and had a friendly chat with him. He said he hoped GEN Lentsov and his wife would visit America some time and that he'd like to invite them to his home. This captain turned out to be one of my listeners when I interpret at the morning telephone conferences.

That evening GEN Lentsov, Marina, Major Bushyhead, and I were invited to dinner with COL Gregory Fontenot at HQ 1st BDE. To get there from Ugljevik we drove through Priboj, Lopare, Celic, Brcko, and Brka, and on southwest. Some of the road SW of Brcko was awfully dusty, which was hard on Bushyhead and his driver in the Humvee following Lentsov's Uazik.

It was a cordial but long evening. On the way back Lentsov insisted we stop and have beer and Coke at an outdoor cafe in Brcko. That was at midnight and there were still a lot of people on the street. Brcko is a site of tension because it was heavily Muslim before the war, but is now occupied almost exclusively by Serbs. But many Muslims want to come back and the Dayton Agreement left the ultimate status of the city to be decided. Brcko is in the northeast of the 1 BDE AOR, not far from the NW boundary of the RUS BDE AOR, and we and the Russians occasionally run joint patrols through the city so as to be seen together. That may have been Lentsov's idea for the stop at the cafe, too.

It was 0100 when we reached Ugljevik.

Sunday evening GEN Lentsov, Marina, and I had dinner with GEN Nash at TAB. That was less strenuous and we returned earlier.

Monday GEN Lentsov, Major Bushyhead, and I attended the brigade commanders' conference, held this time at Camp Guardian just west of Tuzla. I always dread this particular conference because it seems to go on endlessly and I am supposed to whisper a running translation into Lentsov's ear, something I don't do very well. I'm lucky to get the main points.

Tomorrow U.S. Army Chief of Staff GEN Reimer and also some Russian VIPs are visiting.

Thurs, 23 May 96 1000

GEN Lentsov told me some of the details of the soldier's electrocution.

The soldier was on guard duty at motor pool, just the other side of their communications vans. A wire feeding 220 V electricity to the comms vans went across the wire fence around the motor pool. Unnoticed by anyone, the insulation rubbed off and electrified the fence. Nothing happened as long as it was dry, but last week we had several days of rain. The soldier on guard duty was supposed to come around and make periodic reports from inside the motor pool from a field telephone at a corner of the motor pool. But at 2240 on the fatal day the soldier instead reached through the fence from the outside, picked up the phone, made his report, and put the phone down. Then somehow he touched the fence with both hands, and that's how they found him about 40 minutes later. The soldier was 20 years old.

Fri, 24 May 96 1030

Yesterday was a complicated day because RUS BDE had to accomplish at least four things more or less simultaneously: 1. Receive their ambassador to Yugoslavia and a member of their Parliament; 2. Receive U.S. Army Chief of Staff GEN Reimer and party; 3. Meet their biweekly flight at TAB and see off GEN Lentsov's wife; 4. Conduct their usual operations, the latter being further complicated somewhat by a flare-up at Dugi Dio—evidently the Serbs burned down or blew up several Muslim homes.

The biggest event of the day was GEN Reimer's visit. He arrived late and the Russian and American briefings scheduled for him had to be skipped, but the Russians had five APCs of various models lined up in the parking lot plus a light weapons exhibit. After that a Russian spetsnaz (Special Forces) platoon put on a show of hand-to-hand combat that was pretty impressive. Then GEN Reimer and party were escorted across the "Indiana Jones Memorial Bridge" across the "Elba" to the American encampment, from where after a brief visit they boarded their helicopters and left.

GEN Lentsov's wife had departed for TAB earlier by Uazik. The Russian plane was to leave TAB at 1400. At 1350, before Reimer and party had left, Lentsov, Bushyhead, and I piled into a helicopter and busted butt for TAB. Usually the flight is 15 minutes or more, but we made it in ten, landing next to the Russian IL-76. Major Bushyhead ran up in front of it and waved to the pilots, who had a door opened and ladder lowered so Lentsov could say goodbye to his wife.

Today RUS BDE is expecting a visit by Aleksandr Ivanovich Ryabov, Chairman of the Defense Security Committee of the Russian Council of the Federation (the rough equivalent of the Senate Armed Services Committee) and COL GEN Belyaev, Chief of Staff of the Russian Airborne Forces, of which the RUS BDE is a part. GEN Nash is supposed to arrive here by helicopter at 1400 and

94

take them to an American checkpoint and encampment somewhere in 2nd BDE, I think, to show them what our forces in the field look like, with return scheduled at 1600. It is a beautiful, clear spring day, so visually at least it should be splendid. I don't expect to go because they have their own interpreter.

There is a suspicion that the Muslims in Dugi Dio were blowing up already damaged homes of their own in order to blame it on the Serbs and attract our attention and sympathy.

Tues, 28 May 96 1030

GEN Nash did come out Friday afternoon to meet the Russian Parliamentary delegation, together with GEN Cherrie. First thing was dinner at the Russian generals' mess, at which I, as usual, interpreted. A jolly good time was had by all.

Actually, prior to that I had interpreted at the interview a British and a French journalist did with delegation leader Mr. Ryabov. Mr. Ryabov, and I suppose I should have known that, is governor of the Tambov [tahm-BOHF] Region (oblast' [OH-bluhst]), which is why he is a member of the Council of the Federation, Parliament's upper house, the members of which are regional governors, autonomous republic presidents, etc. He turned out to be an entirely affable person, easy to talk to.

After dinner, GEN Nash went on his way and the members of the Russian delegation and I piled into GEN Cherrie's helicopter and went for a ride. Basically, we flew the 75 km (46 miles) of the ZOS which falls in the Russian AOR, flew around the Brcko bridge a couple of times and over Brcko, with special emphasis on the ruined SW side of town, and down SW to Camp McGovern, HQ of LTC Cucolo's battalion in 1 BDE. At Camp McGovern those delegates who were interested crawled into and over an Abrams tank. There were lots of smiles, handshakes, and

95

pictures being taken all over. The son of one of the delegates is a Russian Army helicopter pilot, so he had something to talk about with our helicopter pilot. Again, a splendid time was had by all. GEN Cherrie remarked that he guessed he's now qualified to be a tour leader.

The flap today is the interview two Serbian journalists were supposed to have had with GEN Nash this morning, but which didn't take place.

A new magazine called *Panorama* has started up in Bijeljina, the major city in the NE corner of Bosnia and Herzegovina. In issue number one there is an article about COL Fontenot and an interview with GEN Lentsov. My impression from scanning the first issue is that politically the magazine is moderate. Now the editor, Slobodan Markovic, wants very much to do an interview with GEN Nash.

A tentative date was set and GEN Nash's adjutant was supposed to make the arrangements. But he dropped the ball somehow, and we had to make apologies for that. Then the interview was scheduled for 1000 today at TAB. The question was how to get Mr. Markovic and colleague to TAB, which is in Muslim territory. Markovic was reluctant simply to try to drive in his own car, with its Bijeljina and Republika Srpska license plates. Major Bushyhead didn't feel he could lay on a four-vehicle American convoy specially for this purpose. He asked Russian Chief-of-Staff Soloviev to have a Russian Uazik take them in, but late yesterday Soloviev decided he couldn't do that. The understanding at the end of the day was that Markovic would have to drive in himself, but just the same he should come by here at 0730 for final confirmation of his appointment with GEN Nash.

Markovic and companion were here as instructed. We tried again to get a Russian vehicle and driver, but failed. Then they through us asked the Russians to detail an officer to travel with them in their vehicle. Again the answer was no (reasonably enough, I think). Detailing an American was out of the question—that would be a BIG violation of the force protection rules. All this coming and going and telephoning was complicated by the absence of a Serbian interpreter (ours left for a few days last night). (I can formulate questions with the help of my little Russian-Serbian dictionary, but I have trouble understanding answers.) Finally the Russians' Serbian interpreter showed up and that did help some, esp. since he agreed to go with Markovic. Then Russian COL Breslavsky opined to the Serbs that he thought it dangerous for Serbs to travel unescorted in Muslim territory and in effect talked them out of going. Major Bushyhead reported that to GEN Lentsov, who summoned Breslavsky in and gave him hell. Lentsov said it had occurred to him already last night that sure, the Muslims might hassle the Serbian journalists, who might even end up spending a day in jail, but he was sure we could get them out and it would give the Muslims a black eye (esp. since it is they, not the Serbs, who are making a big deal out of freedom of movement (FOM)).

So Markovic has been greatly inconvenienced and still does not have his interview, Breslavsky is mad at Bushyhead, it has been raining drearily since last night, two other Russian colonels were shouting at each other in the hall this morning, and COL Shamilin just told me that if when I asked him yesterday afternoon whether he would be going to TAB early this morning I had added the reason why it was important, he would have changed his schedule to accommodate. I don't remember exactly, but either I was interpreting for Major Bushyhead or else time was pressing and I couldn't elaborate at the time. Plus when Major Bushyhead instructs me to do something, he usually wants me to do exactly that, neither less nor more, and I have gotten in the habit (have now been trained, in effect) of doing just that.

Fri, 31 May 96 1000

SACEUR GEN Joulwan, his deputy for Russian Forces GEN Shevtsov, and COMEAGLE GEN Nash were just here. GEN Lentsov and I met GEN Joulwan and transported him across the river by Uazik to the Russian parade ground, where Russian soldiers were standing in formation. GEN Joulwan gathered them around him and made a little speech, basically a pep talk. Then Joulwan and Lentsov walked past RUS BDE HQ, across the "Indiana Jones Memorial Bridge," through the American camp, and out to the helicopters, which GENs Joulwan and Nash boarded and left. I interpreted throughout. GEN Shevtsov, who had driven from TAB, remains for a couple of days.

GEN Shevtsov was at the Marshall Center yesterday and brought all of us from there greetings from everybody at the Marshall Center.

1850

My work day today began at 0700 (0730 if you count breakfast at the American mess tent), will not end until some time after 2000 because Friday evenings Chief of Staff LTC Soloviev talks with Chief of Staff Brown at HQ 1 AD at 2000 and with 1st and 2nd BDE XOs either before or after that. It's true I had an hour's sleep this afternoon, as I fairly frequently do after dinner at the Russian dining hall at 1400. Tomorrow morning there is to be a practice alert, for which Major Bushyhead and I are to be at RUS BDE HQ at 0550. So I'll set the alarm for 0500; otherwise I won't have a chance to wash and shave in the morning as we are leaving for TAB NLT 0730 as GEN Nash is meeting with GEN Shevtsov there for an hour before Shevtsov leaves for Brussels and I have to be available to interpret.

2105
Wrapping up.

Sun, 2 Jun 96 0930

GEN Lentsov told me this morning that even the final decision on his replacement, who is due in in about a month, is on hold until after the Russian presidential elections, the first round of which is scheduled for 16 June.

Once a week, most recently on Saturdays, an American convoy from Ugljevik goes in to TAB, leaving at 0730 and not returning until evening, in order to give our soldiers a chance to go to the PX and to search out such entertainment as can be found at TAB.

I went with them yesterday because GEN Shevtsov prior to his return to SHAPE was to spend an hour with GEN Nash and it was expected that I would be the interpreter, as indeed proved to be the case.

After that and a visit to the PX there wasn't anything else I wanted to do at TAB and I managed to hitch a ride back to Ugljevik with COL Goryansky, Chief Logistics Officer at RUS BDE.

GEN Lentsov thinks that order is going to be reestablished in Russia fairly soon. A boss (khozyain [hah-ZYAH-een]) [that's what Stalin was called] will appear and take charge, and in a year or two the country will be on its feet. I don't think he means Zyuganov and I'm certain he doesn't mean Yeltsin, who is going to be done in by Chechnya if nothing else. That leaves GEN (Retired) Aleksandr Lebed as candidate for strong man. Lebed was with the Soviet (later Russian) Airborne Forces through most of his career, as has been Lentsov, and they have even served together. But it isn't just Lentsov who sees Lebed (his name means "Swan") as a possible strong man; such talk began some time ago, more than a year ago. Right now I'm reading Lebed's autobiography, which has already made its way around HQ RUS BDE. Last night on Russian Channel One TV the notorious TV journalist Aleksandr Nevzorov did a special on Lebed; I think it went the better part of an hour.

Nevzorov is notorious because he is a Great Russian chauvinist (Latvians, Lithuanians, Georgians, and others should have been grateful to be part of the Russian Empire and if they weren't grateful—tough), because his ethics are doubtful (his reporting of events in Tbilisi, Georgia in April 1990 and Vilnius, Lithuania in January 1991 was full of lies,

I think), and because of his obvious fascination with necrophilia.

Lebed, I think, is honest and not nearly as extreme in his views as Nevzorov, and I have thought for some time that worse variants are possible. Mainly I'm afraid Lebed would be inclined to forceful, oversimplified solutions, I'm not sure how human rights, freedom of speech, etc would fare, and he himself probably has little understanding of what makes an economy work. On the other hand, I think he has a strong sense of human dignity, both for himself and for others.

A quote from Lebed's book: "The last laugh goes to the one who shoots first." [p.100]

Wed, 5 June 96 0945

Naturally, I like to adduce reasons why I am important to the mission (see, for example, the Sunday Section of *Stars and Stripes*, Sun, 2 June 96).

Day before yesterday the SF guys (all of whom are newly arrived replacements) went to considerable effort to tear down their old tent, which was too small and unbearably hot and stuffy in hot weather, and to put up a new, bigger one. What they didn't know was that GEN Lentsov had long planned to put in a medical facility right where they had put the new tent. So yesterday they tore down the new tent and put it up a few feet away as agreed upon by them and GEN Lentsov. Then somehow Lentsov got the idea that the SF guys' general might get the idea that relations were bad between Lentsov and the new guys and that it was the new guys' fault. So about 1700 yesterday Lentsov took me over to talk to the SF guys. Their previous leader, CPT Alexander Jarotsky, speaks Russian fairly well; none of the new guys speak it very well (just enough to have God-awful misunderstandings). The new SF leader, CW1 Dennis Oglesby, pointed out that in the new location one side of the tent was right next to a cesspool hole. Lentsov pondered that and then said, "Tear it down and put it back up where it was before!" Oh, groan, not again! The SF guys weren't sure whether Lentsov was joking or jerking their chain or what. So after Lentsov left, I stayed awhile and explained that Lentsov was absolutely serious in not wanting them to get in trouble with their general and that for the sake of that and in light of the cesspool hole problem he had told his own medical people, headed by a LTC, to suck it up. But if I hadn't done a reasonably good job of interpreting in the first place and then stayed on to give the SF guys a full explanation and to put my credibility on the line to assure them that Lentsov meant them only the best, there could have been a misunderstanding and hard feelings.

GEN Lentsov has his own interpreters, but he invariably calls on me when he has sensitive things to discuss with the Americans.

Visitors.

Sunday Chief of Staff Soloviev hosted British Brigadier GEN Cook and party at HQ RUS BDE. GEN Cook is Operations Officer at HQ ARRC. He was accompanied by COL Kane, Operations Officer at HQ 1 AD.

After the usual briefing, at which I interpreted, our visitors were dragged up to the Russian steam bath and subjected to that. Actually, it's pretty nice—about 10 minutes in the steam and then a dip in a cold water pool. I can see myself going there voluntarily.

After that came lunch. Although it had been specified ahead of time that they had to leave at 1400 to go on to 1 BDE and therefore they couldn't partake of any alcohol, hardly any Russian is ever going to let you off that easily and of course Soloviev didn't, although he didn't press very much on them. All in all, a little awkward, although gratitude and pleasure were expressed all around multiple times.

Which reminds me of the horror on Carl Bildt's face as he saw the way the Russians proposed to drink the fine Swedish whiskey he had given them. I thought it was funny, but maybe it's not, really. I must say that Americans usually handle these situations better than that. That is, our guys usually say, in effect, "Oh, well, what the hell." (And get denounced in the *Army Times* accompanied by big color pictures.) And the Russians like us for that.

Yesterday's visit was by Deputy SecDef Lodall. GEN Lentsov did the briefing and handled the questions, both of which were pretty extensive. Again I interpreted. One of Mr. Lodall's questions was as to Russian capabilities to move troops and equipment. GEN Lentsov replied that that was no problem as they had acquired quite a lot of experience at it since perestroika [pee-ree-STROY-kuh]. Only GEN Nash seemed to recognize the allusion (Russian withdrawal from Eastern Europe and esp. from East Germany).

After the briefing there was a short tour of the post and a meal without alcohol (it wasn't even noon yet), and the group left, to the disappointment of Major Bushyhead, who didn't get to give a briefing he had worked hard to prepare.

Tonight we go to GEN Nash's going-away dinner for GEN Cherrie.

My own stay in Bosnia may or may not be nearly over depending on the answers to some technical questions about overtime, pay caps, and possible employment by contract through a private company while on Leave Without Pay from Civil Service employment.

Fri, 7 Jun 96 1015

Russian executive office doors are not the same as American executive office doors. Basically, if an American office door is open, you can come in. If it's closed, you have to knock and wait to be invited to enter. With Russians, at least at HQ RUS BDE, the door is always closed. If you need to see the Chief of Staff or the Brigade Commander, you knock on the door, open it, poke your head in and try to judge whether what's going on in the room is more important than your business. You try to catch the boss's eye and act accordingly. It's a workable system, just different.

The going-away dinner for GEN Cherrie went very well. It was held in a large room that was jam-packed with invited guests. The four generals at the head table were, right to left from in behind the table GENS O'Neal, Nash, Cherrie, and Lentsov.

GEN Cherrie has seen major action. He was severely wounded in Vietnam, losing his right leg below the knee and his thumb and two fingers on his right hand plus other injuries from stepping on a mine, was VII Corps operations officer in Desert Storm, began scouting Bosnia for 1 AD and the Allied Rapid Reaction Corps (ARRC) in 1993, and has been Deputy Commander for Maneuvers 1 AD since 1 AD has been in Bosnia. His new assignment is as Chief of Staff for Training at the big Army school at Ft. Leavenworth, Kansas.

GEN Lentsov read his presentation to GEN Cherrie in English plus remarks in Russian and got louder clapping than any of the others making presentations.

My greatest frustration was that I couldn't get my plastic knife to cut my steak.

1345

Yesterday's monthly 1 AD medical conference was held at RUS BDE. I think abut 30 people came and good will abounded.

Today's visitor (so far) has "only" been COL Green, CDR 205th MI Brigade.

[I was on R&R for two weeks at the end of June and the very beginning of July.]

Fri, 5 July 96 0900

It is just infuriating. I tried hard to call home yesterday morning and again later in the day and now this morning. It's easy to get through to Germany, but yesterday even when the phone would ring, no operator would answer and the best I can get this morning is a busy signal.

103

Since both Major Bushyhead and Major Kershaw [Major Bushyhead's prospective replacement] need to be in the office [and there wasn't really room for three in that office], I'm on call on the American side and am either at the Tactical Operations Center (TOC), in the chow hall tent, or in the living quarters tent. The best guess is that Major Bushyhead will leave on or before 23 July, which is when GEN Lentsov leaves.

The trip down from Landsberg AB (a German Air Force base just west of Munich) via German Air Force C-160 on Wed, 3 July 96 was fine. There were just two of us and little or no freight on the plane to Zagreb, where a bunch of people boarded. Arrival at TAB was at 1100, where CPT Ans (a FAO recently arrived from the Marshall Center) met me. Early in the afternoon I caught a ride in a Uazik to RUS BDE.

SecDef Perry, Admiral Smith, GEN Nash, and others were here yesterday. I interpreted at GEN Lentsov's briefing and for his remarks after he was awarded the Legion of Merit medal. I did all right, I guess, but I wasn't in top form. Today would have been better.

Wednesday at TAB GEN Nash greeted me merrily and said the two evenings at his house had been great [GENs Nash and Lentsov and I left TAB by C-12 (a small Army turboprop passenger plane) for Heidelberg and Bad Kreuznach on Sunday, 16 June; we attended a V Corps conference in Heidelberg on Mon, 17 June; on Tues, 18 June they returned to Bosnia and I went home to Garmisch on leave; Sunday and Monday evenings GEN Lentsov spent as guest of GEN Nash at his home; I interpreted throughout]. I showed GEN Nash the pictures I took at his home and at Heidelberg and he asked for a set. GEN Lentsov should have a set, too.

Mon, 8 July 96 1230

I'm afraid it's going to be a long, hot summer—literally. Even with fans the tent I live in is unbearable by noon. The best place I've found for midday is a bunker where there is shade and pretty good air circulation.

Of course that's for the time being, until Major Bushyhead leaves, which should be NLT the 23rd.

Since my return last Wednesday I have continued living on the American side (by choice—there is room in the dorm building on the other side) and hanging out here for most of the day so that Major Kershaw can be in the office with Major Bushyhead. When Major Bushyhead leaves I expect to go back to the office.

Yesterday morning, though, Major Bushyhead went to TAB for the day, so I spent all morning at the office. Then at noon I was invited to go to Bijeljina with SF CWO Dennis Oglesby to attend some "Feed the Children" function at Nedeljko (Chicago Ned) Todorovic's Chicago Raj [pronounced "Rye"] (Paradise) Restaurant. We were there until 2030. [CWO Oglesby has a risk-taker personality.]

I should have written about Chicago Ned long ago. He showed up to call on Major Bushyhead just a few days after we arrived in mid-January. He is a huge man probably in his early 50's. He went to the U.S. in the 1960's, says he made a pile and got to know a lot of people. Got U.S. citizenship. But he says he can't get a U.S. living permit for his new wife, so he is more or less stuck here. [He was wearing a VRS (Vojska Republike Srpske—Army of the Republika Srpska) uniform the first time I saw him.] He says he tries to be the support for about 150 orphans at an orphanage. He gets some help from Serbs in the U.S. and from charities and contributors, but help is falling off because the war is over. There is a British office of "Feed the Children" in Bijeljina and their representative was there as well as several people from the British military mission in Bijeljina. Recently one of the orphans, a 13-year-old boy, hanged himself, evidently from despair. Rebecca ..., the

105

British representative from "Feed the Children," said there are 50,000 refugees in Bijeljina [at least half the population of the town] and that the situation is very grim, even if it doesn't look too bad just riding down the street. Rebecca speaks Russian and a year or two ago was working for "Feed the Children" in Georgia (the one in the Caucasus), where she says it was far worse than it is here now.

The Lebed autobiography was returned to my desk, so I'm finishing that now.

American Army engineers are putting up barriers around the front and side perimeter, to ward off truck bombs, I assume. We are already protected by sandbags closer up from anyone who might try to shoot at us from the road.

Thurs, 11 July 96 1000

The last couple of days have been cool with some rain. [And in general the summer didn't turn out nearly as hot as I'd expected.]

The new Russian CDR is due in tomorrow and GEN Nash has invited him to dinner Sunday. So I'll get some action.

1300

Some European journalists were here day before yesterday, and after COS LTC Soloviev briefed them, GEN Lentsov talked with them a few minutes. He said some pretty quotable things about NATO and Russo-American cooperation. AFN has been broadcasting it, I'm told, and GEN Nash mentioned it at this morning's telephone conference. I sure hope I got it right and wasn't misquoted. And/or it may have come from the recording one of the journalists made of GEN Lentsov speaking.

Sun, 14 July 96 0945

Two Russian planes came into TAB Friday. Major rotation of troops is taking place. COL Generalov, GEN Lentsov's replacement, arrived plus COL GEN Podkolzin, CDR of Russian Airborne Forces, and COL GEN Shevtsov, SACEUR GEN Joulwan's Deputy for Russian forces, are visiting. Yesterday we went back to TAB with them for the 1800 briefing and dinner afterwards. Everybody seemed to be having a good time.

GEN Nash called me in for a short talk before the briefing. He wanted to know what the feeling was for the new RUS BDE CDR, but I could only say that it was still too early and I had no feeling for it yet, but he seems fine. COL Generalov is even taller than GEN Lentsov, about 6'2" or 6'3", I suppose, not heavy in the upper body like Lentsov, with boxer's nose. A rough-hewn man, but not flamboyant like Lentsov. GEN Nash wanted my judgment on Lentsov's sincerity, and I said I believed in it and that I have 100% confidence in Lentsov's integrity; after all at a moment when I needed help and protection, I went unhesitatingly straight to Lentsov, which I think can also be taken as evidence of the success of GEN Nash's policy.

Tues, 16 July 96 0930

In spite of efforts and promises, I don't think we will ever get the *Stars and Stripes* regularly. [We never did.]

I am reading Major Kershaw's copy of *Stalin* by Eduard Radzinsky. Aside from one stupid mistake by the translator, probably compounded by the computer, it is excellent. The interpreter confused Gor'kii, usually transliterated as Gorky, the city named after the writer and in the 1920's still called Nizhnii (or Nizhny) Novgorod, with Gorki, the estate near Moscow where Lenin lived the last years of his life and died, so everywhere one would expect Gorki one finds Nizhnij (or Nizhny) Novgorod. There is no indication that the book has been published in Russian in Russia, but if it hasn't, it should be. [It has been.]

If Nika is interested in pain as an intellectual proposition, she might like the book. Bukharin's letters to Stalin begging for his life are especially painful.

Wed, 17 July 96 0900

COL Fontenot came to dinner yesterday, arriving at 1730. He was introduced to the new RUS BDE CDR and marched up the hill to the *banya* [BAH-nyuh], the Russian steam bath. You spend about five minutes, or as much as you can stand, in the steam room, which is mainly terrifically hot air, or like a sauna, without much humidity, and then come out and jump into a pool of cool water, and then back into the steam room (the *parilka* [pah-REEL-kuh]). Last night we did this maybe half a dozen times, showered, and went still wearing our sheets into a room where supper was laid out. They didn't spare the vodka, either.

Besides COL Fontenot, GEN Lentsov, and COL Generalov, a GEN (one-star) Rybkin was present. The steam bath was refreshing and pleasant and the meal was good. But the best thing was the socializing. I don't know how they understood each other, because they kept starting new sentences before I could get the previous one finished, but everyone was very jolly, proclaiming fealty, etc. The substance wasn't in the literal meaning of what people were trying to say, anyway. But I have already mentioned how well COL Fontenot and GEN Lentsov hit it off. Things will be fine with Generalov, too.

One serious point that was made was that the Russian Airborne have seen a lot of action since 1979 (Afghanistan, Azerbaijan, Abkhazia, and elsewhere) and are still seeing it (Chechnya) and they are sick of seeing disfigured women's and children's corpses (plus those of their and the enemy's soldiers) and don't want any more of it. They much prefer being interposed together with Americans between former warring parties like here in Bosnia and keeping the peace.

The dinner ended about 2100.

COL Generalov wants me to help him learn English and has sent to Moscow for materials. (His foreign language was German.) [He does seem to have a lot of talent for language-learning; he is quick at picking up English words and phrases.]

Several of our soldiers want me to help them get started with Russian.

COL Generalov rather expects the Russians to be invited to stay on in Bosnia, in which case his tour will be for a year, which seems to suit him fine.

COL Generalov is 37, but looks older, maybe because he's nearly bald.

Thurs, 18 July 96 0745

Yesterday we were visited by a group of Russian TV, radio, and print journalists representing RTV (Russian 2nd Channel TV), Mayak (radio), and the newspapers *Segodnya* [see-VOH-dnyuh], *Izvestia,* and *Krasnaya Zvezda.* No translation was necessary.

GEN Lentsov spoke at length and what he had to say was interesting.

Mainly he tends to think Franjo Tudjman and Alija Izetbegovic are about as guilty as Radovan Karadzic and Mladic and anyway how can one seriously contemplate the arrest of the leaders of an undefeated side? [One, I would think, does not necessarily follow from the other.] And the negative consequences could be considerable.

0915

After the briefing there was some free time, and I talked some to the Mayak representative. He recorded an interview with me and with an American female major, for whom I interpreted. [Females in the American Army are always a mystery to the Russians.]

GEN Lentsov had emphasized how well Russian-American cooperation is working out and everything everybody else had to say was consistent with that (because it's the truth).

Fri, 19 July 96 1000

GEN Nash, GEN O'Neal, and all 1 AD Brigade CDRs, including the Nord-Pole and Turkish Brigades, came to GEN Lentsov's going-away dinner early yesterday evening. A great time was had by all, but the vodka flowed more sparingly than on 23 Feb. GEN Nash commented on that to me, with special reference to the pictures, letters, and articles in the *Army Times*. Actually, after the main American party left, evidently the vodka did flow pretty freely, because some people are feeling awful this morning.

GEN Sorokin, chief of the Vukosavci Operational Group, is being replaced by GEN Khalilov (the rotation there is every ninety days). GEN Khalilov's 25-year-old daughter, a tall, slim, and strikingly pretty young woman, is an officer with the Russian Battalion in Eastern Slavonia, and was present yesterday. When I left about 2030 Major Kershaw was talking to her. Later, he says, GEN Khalilov told his daughter to get away from him (Major Kershaw). I must say that Russian paratrooper BDUs don't do the horrible things to women's figures that American BDUs do.

The Russians also presented Major Bushyhead with a going-away plaque, letter of thanks, etc. Major Bushyhead is to be XO at a 2 BDE 1 AD battalion in Baumholder, Germany.

GEN Nash wants me to get addresses on GEN Lentsov so that he won't lose track of him in the coming years. I have an idea I'll be involved in that to some extent from time to time. I don't want to lose track of Lentsov, either, for that matter.

GEN Lentsov leaves the 23rd. That morning he is to spend an hour or so "just the three of us: you, me (GEN Nash), and Jim." Same thing that afternoon or the next day with COL Generalov.

GEN Shevtsov has said at least once that he thinks GEN Nash should be appointed NATO representative to the Russian Ministry of Defense in Moscow and GEN Nash has said that GEN Lentsov could be the future if not President of Russia, than at least its Minister of Defense. Since Lentsov is only 39, certainly the position of MOD is possible.

COL Generalov's father at one time commanded all Soviet ground forces in Afghanistan. I don't know whether that's a recommendation or not. GEN Rodionov, just appointed MOD, is also from the Airborne, as I understand it. Lebed in his book *Za derzhavu obidno* (I Feel Bad For The Country) denies that Rodionov slaughtered civilians in Tbilisi, Georgia, in April 1990.

GEN Lentsov and also GEN Rybkin say that their prime instruction in Afghanistan was to avoid loss of their own soldiers. And it's true that their losses were only about a third of ours in Vietnam (about 15,000 against about 50,000), but a direct comparison may or may not be valid.

COL Generalov was asked what would happen if we were shot at from the trees across the road and above the American encampment, and his answer was that a few minutes later there wouldn't be any trees left there. So he doesn't think anyone will try such a thing.

Some IFOR jets flew over pretty loudly an hour or so ago. That seems to have been in response to some remarks by certain Bosnian Serb officials.

At the same time today the Russians and we are making great efforts to get the cousin of the Bosnian Serbian army's liaison officer to the Russians to the funeral this afternoon of the cousin's mother on Muslim-Croat Federation territory. The Serbian Majevicka [mah-yeh-VEECH-kah] Brigade commander, whose HQ is just across the parking lot-parade grounds, was in and out all morning on the issue

111

and since his Russian is functional, I got involved talking with him, too.

No Serb, after all, walks around carrying a sign saying, "I'm a war criminal," and yet I, at least, wonder from time to time who I'm really looking at and sometimes talking to.

1350

I was just talking to COL Shamilin, one of the Russian liaison officers to the FWPs. He thinks things could get darned interesting well before the elections (tentatively scheduled for 14 Sep 96). He's staying until the end (Dec-Jan), "unless I get scared and decide to run." He says the IPTF in Bijeljina are in a panic over threats the Serbs have made, but that the IPTF in Zvornik, close to Mladic's HQ, are calm. One of them says, "Heck, you get $500 a day for being a hostage—I'll go."

COL Shamilin thinks the FWPs could have hostilities under way in a matter of hours, albeit without heavy weapons, since those are in storage. I asked COL Shamilin what we (IFOR) would do in the event of renewed war, and he said darned if he knew. Maybe I should be doing PT, in case I have to run. If IFOR ever does detain Karadzic or Mladic, things will get AWFULLY tense at the least. But as long as they are at large, they'll act as spoilers to prevent real peace and establishment of real democracy, freedom of the media, etc., on their territory.

On a calmer note, GEN Nash told COL Generalov yesterday that after the September elections here, when things have calmed down, he'll arrange a conference to go to in Germany like the one he, I, and Lentsov went to in June. [It never happened.]

Mon, 22 July 96 0930

I'm flying in to TAB with GEN Lentsov to see GEN Nash this afternoon.

Wed, 24 July 96 0900

The big event yesterday was seeing GEN Lentsov off at TAB. GEN Shevtsov, GEN Joulwan's Deputy at SHAPE for Russian forces, arrived on the same plane. He went on at length to GEN Nash with a Russian media microphone (NTV) in his nose about how Russia, the U.S., and NATO have to be together, how great GEN Nash is, and mainly that he will not allow the Russian BDE to participate in tracking down Karadzic and Mladic.

Major Bushyhead leaves TAB today. He took me aside and said just the same we had participated in history, which is absolutely true. The evening before the Russians at Ugljevik had put on a big dinner for him, which I think was appropriate.

The GAO is supposed to be here this morning.

The American encampment here is being turned into a fortress.

1815

I thought the GAO inquiry awfully superficial.

Meetings with GENs Nash, Shevtsov, Belyaev, and Khalilov tomorrow together with COL Generalov, then helicopter overflights Friday.

Sun, 28 July 96 1130

Thursday morning we went to TAB to meet COL GEN Shevtsow, who was flying in from Moscow. We had a little flap at the beginning when COL Generalov forgot to tell us he was leaving and it was only several minutes later that Major Kershaw and I realized that Generalov had left. The thing is that American military personnel in American military vehicles are not allowed to travel one vehicle at a time. The general rule requires minimum four-vehicle convoys, one exception being that a single American vehicle can travel if it is with at least one other IFOR, but non-American, vehicle. But if we showed up with just our

Humvee at the gate to TAB, there would be trouble. So SGT Andrew Carter (my 6'7" former "bodyguard") poured on the coal and we went chasing after COL Generalov's Uazik. Our Humvee is a "ragtop," as it were, and so lighter than other Humvees, but with the same engine and suspension. I.e., pretty firm riding at normal speeds. But at 90 kph or so (approx. 60 mph) it swallows humungous potholes pretty well. Turns out that with SGT Carter at the wheel it can be set into pretty nice four-wheel drifts on mountain roads, too. None of us, naturally, strapped in. So it was the most exciting ride I've had on the road to Tuzla since the first trip in with (then) COL Lentsov and his inexperienced driver through the snow in early February. We caught up with the Uazik, which was traveling pretty slowly, about two thirds of the way in. Afterwards COL Generalov told us that he had remembered us, but only after he was already under way.

A UH-60 Blackhawk helicopter picked up me and COL Generalov Friday morning at 0855 and took us to TAB, where GEN Nash got on. We were than flown to the NORDPOL (Nordic-Polish) BDE HQ not very far away for a service for Polish corporal Mieczyslaw Szternik [myeh-CHIH-swahf] [SHTEHR-neek], who was killed in a road accident on Wed.

After that we flew to a helicopter scout squadron south of TAB commanded by LTC Harriman. The briefing for COL Generalov there was interpreted by an American Army staff sergeant whose Russian is excellent. GEN Nash asked me how good he was and I said, "Excellent. Sounds just like me!" GEN Nash then said, "Great. That means I can fire you." I wanted to say, "Golly, I sure wish you would," but I didn't. [Because then I could have gone on a marvelous vacation to the States.] Turned out the fellow had spoken Ukrainian as a child, which gave him a leg up on Russian. And he has a barely perceptible accent in English. But he has put a lot of effort into his Russian—he sounded like an American, not a Ukrainian, speaking Russian. He has all the structures under control, excellent pronunciation, and

114

extensive vocabulary. I did get the feeling he doesn't have my colloquial range, but I think his knowledge of terminology is better than mine. His name is Victor Kamenir.

From there we flew back to TAB to meet Blues singer B.B. King as he arrived about 1330. From there we flew hell and gone SW to the Glomac bomb range in the British (?) sector. Took an hour to get there. The terrain is dramatically different: high, sparsely populated, dry and bare with rocky outcroppings. Helicopters and artillery were firing into a hillside with simulated air strikes from A-10 Warthogs. The scenario was a Klingon attack by GEN Englertovic (1 AD 2 BDE XO is LTC Englert) onto Romulan territory across a ZOS (Zone of Separation) in violation of a NATO-enforced peace to which NATO is responding. A Bosnian Muslim observer showed; unfortunately, his Bosnian Serb counterpart did not, since a part of the intent no doubt was to impress.

It was 1800 when we got back to TAB, in time for the last half hour or so of the B.B. King concert. I thought the music would have been just great about 20 DB lower, say at about 120 DB.

I'll have to ask Nika whether I should feel anointed for having been in the presence of B.B. King.

Our helicopter crew had gone out for pizza when COL Generalov and I were ready to go, but GEN Nash's driver (Todd Hamilton(?)) and adjutant (CPT Carlyle) were able to get us a ride on another one and we arrived back at Ugljevik at 1930. I was pretty tired by then and grateful to Major Kershaw that he had arranged for a Russian interpreter to handle the Friday evening Chief of Staff conference call.

Yesterday morning we were back at TAB at 1000 for a brigade CDRs' conference. The September elections were the main topic.

A new Russian interpreter was translating for COL Generalov until he hung up on something and I was called up. In a way I had set the guy up because I hate interpreting at such conferences, and when COL Generalov had hesitated to put his man in, I said, "Sure, let him do it." And when

GEN Nash asked whether he could handle it, I said, "I hope so." The fellow's English sounds pretty good, so I think he was probably doing OK, but it is hard because of the acronyms and abbreviations and some American sub-colloquial speech, esp. when GEN Nash is being folksy.

Tues, 30 July 96 0945

Yesterday morning COL Generalov and I set off for TAB thinking we were going to a farewell ceremony for IFOR Commander Admiral Leighton Smith. It turned out to be a welcoming ceremony for BG Casey, GEN Cherrie's replacement, Admiral Smith's ceremony having been shifted to 1445. So now all of COL Generalov's day was to go down the tubes, rather than just half of it.

After the morning ceremony we went to the Russian 1st Battalion garrison at Simin Han. Just before noon word came from Russian 2nd Battalion Checkpoint 34A, north of Celic on the road to Brcko, that a battle was taking place a couple of kilometers from the checkpoint. COL Generalov set out to investigate. He offered to drop me off in Priboj, but I said I preferred to go with him. A truckload of soldiers and a BTR (APC) accompanied us. It turned out that the Americans have a firing range in 1 AD 1 BDE territory close to RUS CP 34A and were firing. The Russians would have known this had they read the firing range schedules sent from Division HQ. On the other hand, if the Americans hadn't been firing routinely from there before, they should have given the Russians a heads-up. The Russians do not have communications equipment in their Uaziks, so the RUS CDR is incommunicado when he is on the road.

So for me and COL Generalov yesterday mainly amounted to two wild goose chases.

COL Generalov is still getting a hold on things at RUS BDE and prefers to stick to business for the time being.

1030

116

One of the most consistently frustrating things throughout here has been the information vacuum. I'm convinced we are NEVER going to get the *Stars and Stripes* regularly [never did]. We now have AFN TV in the chow hall tent, which is fine if you happen to be there at 0700 or 1800 and if American-edition CNN Headline News is your idea of news (same for S&S). The Early Bird is good, but it comes in sporadically and a week or two late. The Russians pull in ORT (Channel 1 TV) (and also RTV, Channel 2 TV), but again you have to be in the room when news is being broadcast; furthermore that is subject to interruptions.

Wed, 31 July 96 0900

The American LNO (Liaison Officer) at HQ RUS BDE gets involved in things like the following:

A week or so ago the ABiH (Army of Bosnia and Herzegovina), i.e. the Muslims, notified HQ 1 AD that on such-and-such a date and at such-and-such a time they wanted to move some weapons from a declared site in the RUS BDE AOR to a site in the 2 BDE 1 AD AOR. HQ 1 AD tasked RUS BDE with escorting the movement and handover to 2 BDE. The Russians, probably with a BTR (APC), which has a two-way radio, and a truckload of soldiers arrived at the ABiH site yesterday at 0700. Before getting under way the Russians (as was their right) demanded a look at what the ABiH was transporting. The ABiH officer in charge said he had no document authorizing that. The Russians reported that back to HQ RUS BDE, which responded that not a wheel was to turn until they had a look at what the ABiH wanted to transport, and, of course, they couldn't move without escort. The Russian Operations Officer brought this to our attention at 1040, wondering what to do next. We informed HQ 1 AD and there the matter stood. By early afternoon HQ 1 AD was expecting more reports, which it wasn't getting, and was getting a little testy. Later we learned that the Russians had hung around the

ABiH site until 1200 and left. Nothing more happened. The Russians at HQ RUS BDE thought that either there had been a failure to coordinate somewhere or that the ABiH had wanted to move something that they didn't want IFOR to know about. My guess would be the former.

A major activity these days is preparation for the Bosnia-wide elections scheduled for 14 September. RUS BDE is to scout the polling places in their AOR, for example. They are also to help the local authorities come up with internationally funded projects that would give quick results, esp. in terms of work for unemployed demobilized soldiers.

COL Generalov evidently regrets the breakup of the geopolitical entity formerly called the "Soviet Union," or at least the Slavic part of it (Great Russia (or simply Russia), Belorussia (Belarus), the Ukraine (once known as "Little Russia," to the irritation of at least some Ukrainians), and maybe the northern areas of Kazakhstan, which are predominantly Russian and Ukrainian in population. Belorussia is already heading back toward union with Russia and COL Generalov says he believes the Ukraine will reunite with Russia within the next four years, although he realizes that the western part of the Ukraine will be against it.

My guess, for what it's worth, is that the Ukraine will never go back if only because once a power structure is in place, people occupying positions of power don't want to give them up. Who wants, in effect, to be governor of a state when he or she can be president of a country?

But COL Generalov is glad to see the Soviet regime gone. His own grandfather was a relatively well-to-do peasant and avoided exile or worse only because he was quick to turn over everything he owned to the collective farm set up where they had lived and had had their land. But they understood that it amounted to the lazy, the incompetent, and the drunks robbing the industrious, competent, and sober— which, incidentally, they didn't get to keep, either, because the State then robbed everybody.

At one of GEN Lentsov's last talks with GEN Nash, he said that he was rethinking some of his positions (he has held both sides equally responsible for the Cold War, in particular). That may be the result of his having recently read my essay on the Cold War that I wrote at the MC in January 95.

Thurs, 1 Aug 96 0930

Representatives of the ECMM (European Community Monitoring Mission), the "Ice Cream Guys," were here yesterday to talk election issues. They were supposed to meet with COL Breslavsky, one of the Russian LNOs to the Serbs, Muslims, and Croats (only there don't seem to be any Croats in the BUS BDE AOR), but had to settle for LTC Isakhanyan, the new Chief of Staff at RUS BDE. Their particular concern centers on the town of Koraj on election day (14 Sep).

Before the war Koraj was predominantly Muslim, although the surrounding countryside was and is completely or nearly completely Serbian. But now Koraj is in Serbian territory and all the Muslims have been driven out. Most of them are refugees in Celic, a town just a few kilometers west of Koraj in Muslim territory. Both are in the RUS BDE sector. According to the Dayton Agreement, people have the right to vote, directly or absentee, at the place they lived before the war. The Serbs in Koraj, many if not most of whom are refugees from Sarajevo and elsewhere, don't want Muslims voting in Koraj. If Muslims come in large numbers (groups of 40 or 50 or more) into the center of Koraj, the local authorities say they fear violence. One proposal is to set up a polling station on the outskirts of town, but the Muslim leadership insists on it being in the center. Neither side wants to back down. The ECMM wants IFOR to enforce the Dayton Agreements by stationing forces at polling places.

LTC Isakhanyan is really against that, and the ECMM representative was getting kind of exasperated, especially when LTC Isakhanyan suggested the Muslims come in groups of two or three. "That'll just get them killed," was the ECMM representative's response. I.e., he sees the Russians caving in entirely to the Serbs to avoid having to enforce the Dayton Agreement with possible attendant violence. LTC Isakhanyan did hasten to say that naturally RUS BDE will carry out orders from superior military authorities.

IFOR sees such enforcement as more of a police function and is trying to shrug it off, to put it on the backs of the international organizations, especially the IPTF (International Police Task Force), while the international organizations rightly point out that only IFOR has the physical capabilities required to enforce the Dayton Agreements.

I think the ethnic nationalists on all sides, but especially the Serbs and only to a slightly lesser extent the Muslims, are going to work their will on their own territories and ethnic divisions will be semi-legitimized in a semi-free and semi-democratic vote.

Sun, 4 Aug 96 1100

We've had some excitement.

On the morning of Thurs, 1 Aug 96, some Muslims from Celic crossed the line between the Muslim-Croat Federation on the west and the Republika Srpska on the east on the road between Celic and Koraj and began cutting grass near the road. The Serbian police and about 20 Serbs from Koraj, some of them armed, showed up on the scene. Representatives from the Russian IFOR company stationed in Koraj were also there, and they and the Serbian police got the Muslims to leave. The Russians confiscated one automatic rifle. The Koraj police detained one elderly Muslim and his horse and cart. The Serbs kept the horse and cart, but released the Muslim to the Russians with the request that they escort him to Celic, which they did. The Muslim had been beaten while in Serbian custody. The keeping of the horse and cart and the beating of the Muslim aroused the indignation of the people of Celic. COL Generalov met with the leaders of Celic and Koraj to try to end the conflict. However, that afternoon two shots were fired, resulting in the wounding and later death of a Muslim, causing further disturbances. [But the Muslims refused to show anybody the body.] The shooting was brought to the attention of COL Generalov only at 2300 and at that by a Serb.

COL Generalov again met with the leaders of Celic and Koraj on the morning of Friday, 2 Aug 96. Both sides assured him that they would keep the situation under control.

The Russians reported what they knew to HQ 1 AD early in the evening of the 1st. But they did not tell us about the shooting until early in the afternoon of the 2nd. The 2nd was a big holiday for the Russians here because it was Airborne Day. COL Generalov had rushed off to Celic-Koraj at 0600 that morning, but nobody could or would tell us why. I concluded that it must be something Russian-internal having to do with the company stationed in Koraj.

The morning of the 2nd we even had trouble getting a Russian in a position of authority to the telephone for GEN Nash's telephone conference at 0830. GEN Nash began with a whole speech about Russian Airborne Day and then I had to say, "Sir, there aren't any Russians in the room right now," while I signaled frantically through the window to Major Kershaw to get someone in there. [It was especially embarrassing because numerous people at HQ 1 AD had reminded GEN Nash what day it was and how great it would be if he would start the morning with a verbal tribute to Russian Airborne Day.]

Airborne Day celebrations took up all the morning of the 2nd.

About 1400 COL Generalov burst into our office and dictated a report which I took down verbatim. After making a clean copy and being unable to locate COL Generalov to confirm that I had it all correct [I did], I dictated an English translation of the report to Major Kershaw, who wrote it down in his journal. Major Kershaw then reported the gist of it to HQ 1 AD. I left the office at 1500 and was gone approximately half an hour.

For reasons unknown to us and which are causing a lot of commotion, the report was not brought to the attention of GEN Nash until 1800 on the 2nd. Reportedly GEN Nash is madder than hell about the delay. Major Kershaw and I spent much of the evening getting further clarifications from the Russians. At 1930 COL Generalov gave an oral report through me by telephone to GEN Nash.

COL Generalov with GEN Nash's approval has taken a number of steps, including round-the-clock patrolling of the road between Celic and Koraj and the setting up of a checkpoint on the road at the IEBL (Inter-Entity Boundary Line).

Four IPTF guys—two Poles, a Russian, and an Irishman—showed up here yesterday morning (the 3rd), saying that a Muslim crowd in Celic had threatened them in their vehicle and in particular had tried to drag one of them (the Polish interpreter, who was in civilian clothes) out of the vehicle and pulled the buttons off the shirt of another of them. The IPTF don't carry arms and feel pretty vulnerable.

A little after 1000 yesterday morning (Sun, 4 Aug 96), GEN Casey (GEN Cherrie's replacement), COL Generalov, and I flew up to Celic- Koraj and set down on the road where the new RUS CP is to be established and near where the incidents had taken place. It was a little tight getting in because of trees on both sides and it took two tries with the Blackhawk. The Russians were VERY emphatic that we were not to land in a field next to the road because of mines. The houses in the area are all war-damaged and vacant and there were a lot of old machine-gun and AK-47 shell casings littering the road.

The Celic police chief was there and talked to COL Generalov through the Russian interpreter Aleksei Bosykh with me interpreting for GEN Casey. The Chief of Police said he wasn't justifying it, but he said that the man who tried to rough up the IPTF was drunk and was the son of the old man the Serbs had beaten and a relative of the one who was killed. Then we drove down the road a way and Russian officers who had been present at the events of the morning of the 1st (the weapons confiscation, the crowd, etc) told GEN Casey through me what they had seen. Then GEN Casey departed and I stayed with COL Generalov, who scouted further for a suitable building to house the HQ for the platoon that will man their CP. SF SSGT Eddie Trumbel was there with a GPS to help reestablish the IEBL markers that had been destroyed. The Celic Chief of Police reappeared and was mad because it looked to him like the Russians were going to set one of the markers so as to deny the Muslims access to a side road. He got pretty heated, and the Russians were clearly irritated, too. That they only understood each other at about 30% didn't help (the interpreter was off elsewhere).

Sometime after 1200 (on a very hot and muggy day) COL Generalov, COL Zaitsev, the new Chief Russian LNO at TAB, another officer, and I set out in a Uazik for Ugljevik via Koraj.

Driving up the street in Koraj, we encountered a young Serb in civilian clothes walking down the street carrying an AK-47 Kalashnikov automatic rifle. We stopped and COL Generalov hopped out, grabbed the rifle, and shoved the young man in the back seat with me and the others. We took him to the HQ of the Russian company in Koraj and turned him over to the Company CDR for further disposition. [The young man appeared a little scared, and even seemed to hope that I could help him.] What will happen (has happened) is that the AK-47 will be confiscated and the young man released. [Out in the country as we neared Ugljevik we encountered an older man in civilian clothes walking down the road also carrying an AK-47. This time Generalov said the hell with it as it would take too much time fussing and we kept on driving.]

Wed, 7 Aug 96 1545

Late Monday afternoon, 5 Aug 96, COL Generalov, GEN Khalilov, CDR of the Vukosavci group, and I flew to TAB to meet with GEN Nash at the Russians' request. Four-star GEN Crouch, CG U.S. ground forces in Europe, was there, which held things up a bit. GEN Nash took me aside and asked what the Russians' agenda was, to which I replied that I thought that they wanted to explain the hang-ups on reporting the Celic-Koraj incidents.

GEN Nash started the meeting by saying that the morning of 2 Aug twenty-two people had reminded him it was Russian Airborne Day plus there were two signs saying so. I.e., it was a BIG deal. So he started the telephone conference that morning with this big speech about it, and when he was all through I tell him in the hearing of dozens of people listening in that no Russian at HQ RUS BDE had heard it.

Anyway, GEN Nash explained that they should report even fragmentary and unverified information immediately, and GEN Khalilov and COL Generalov agreed to do so. No pain there. Then we flew back to Ugljevik. [GEN Khalilov was carrying around the verbatim copy I had made of COL Generalov's statement, so I guess they were satisfied with my secretarial capabilities in Russian.]

That evening Major Kershaw, COL Generalov, and I drove to the airstrip just this side of Bijeljina, where LG Sir Michael J.D. Walker, CDR of the Allied Rapid Reaction Corps, i.e. of NATO and NATO-led ground forces in Bosnia and Herzegovina, has a temporary HQ as he moves around the country getting a feel for things in the pre-election period. It was a very nice evening and I was in good form.

That same evening several of our Camp Ugly soldiers, including two women, were caught just a little way past the camp boundary drinking with some Serbs. So now an investigation is on and it's kind of unpleasant. [Our Serbian interpreter Slobodan "Bob" Mikic [MEE-keech] was with them, which mitigates it just a little.]

124

Yesterday morning Major Kershaw and I drove in to Bijeljina for a meeting GEN Walker had with Dragomir Ljubojevic, Mayor of Bijeljina. Even though it was still morning, as I recall, GEN Walker downed a healthy shot of brandy. Then the Russians hosted him at dinner here, and I doubt he got by with less than six or seven pretty stiff shots (as we measure it) of vodka. Then he had a meeting with the Mayor of Ugljevik, but this time he didn't touch the brandy. Each of these meetings went 1 1/2–2 hours. And he's doing this all over Bosnia, but at least there's only one RUS BDE.

I really like GEN Walker—for one thing, he's well-spoken (as an upper-class Englishman should be) and easy to interpret for. He wants a copy of my book when I write it and I promised to send him a copy (GEN Nash wants one, too). (Of course, it's not going to be a book, just a journal that I think will be of interest only to the most dedicated of those interested in Bosnia [and/or Russo-American military cooperation].)

The Marshall Center is organizing a conference in St. Petersburg, Russia, Sep 21-23 at which GENs Nash, Shevtsov, and Lentsov are to speak. GEN Nash says he plans to take me.

I've been living in the American encampment since 10 June, but I plan to move back over soon. Three women live in the tent I'm in, and all I can say is that it is a LOT less exciting than some fevered imaginations would have it. And the *Stars and Stripes* notwithstanding, if there is any action at Camp Ugly, I certainly don't know about it. It may or may not matter that they're all married. SGT Wise is a computer-comms operator, SGT Wijk [wick] is a medic, and PVT Kelso is a cook. But the latter are here temporarily and it is they who were involved in our incident. Kelso is a German, incidentally [only her accent gives her away].

The Mayor of Ugljevik still had his picture of Karadzic up on the wall. One Serb I know says a lot of Serbs would like to see the end of Koradzic.

Fri, 9 Aug 96 1900

Yesterday somebody in a dark-colored Jeep Cherokee without license plates traveling toward Tuzla stopped on the road near the American encampment and was taking pictures. Today we are warned that terrorists are planning an action against US/IFOR forces in Bosnia and there is even information that some particular truck may be involved. There may or may not be any connection, of course, if only because such an action seems more likely on the Muslim side. Needless to say, we're taking security measures.

East Bosnian Corps Commander (VRS) GEN Gavric met with GEN Nash here for an hour-and-a-half briefing this morning. Their talk was cordial, but businesslike. GEN Nash's two Serbo-Croatian interpreters, CPT Petnicki and SFC Bosnjak, were featured on AFN News last night. SFC Bosnjak was his interpreter today. I translated into Russian for COL Generalov.

GEN Nash asked me whether I'd ever been to St. Petersburg, and I said the last time I was there was in Sep 79, when Allis-Chalmers took its employees there on an excursion from our site in the Ukraine. I hope somebody remembers we all have to have visas.

Sun, 11 Aug 96 1100

I finally moved back over to my old room on the Russian side of the river this morning.

An ICTY (International Court Tribunal for the Former Yugoslavia) team came in Friday and will be with us until Thursday. It consists of a team of four—three women and a man. They are doing advance work. Somebody else will do the digging [at mass grave sites]. Speaking of which, CPT Ans has been invited to an exhumation on Thursday. (Marine CPT Matthew Ans recently switched places with CPT Chuck McLaughlin, i.e. TAB for here.)

126

Division is evidently in an uproar over the terrorist threat. We're a lot calmer about it out here, but we have taken increased security measures. [The reason HQ was in an uproar was not because anybody genuinely feared a terrorist strike, but because if God forbid there should be one, anyone in a position of responsibility who can't prove that he or she did the utmost in advance to protect U.S. forces against such strikes can just kiss off his or her career. A lot of what goes on at any HQ, at least at an American HQ, is done not so much for purposes of mission accomplishment as for purposes of career protection or enhancement. There is less of a tendency toward that in the field, which can be a source of irritation both at HQ and in the field.] To get through the gate to the American encampment from the road already required a sharp right or left turn off the Tuzla-Bijeljina highway. Now in addition to metal and concertina-wire barriers and a sturdy wooden beam, getting through which would make a God-awful noise, they would have to push three or four Humvees out of the way and go across a parking lot before getting anywhere near where people work and sleep and through more sandbag barriers and big metal containers at that.

It would be easier for terrorists with a truck bomb to come in through the Russian front gate [which is nothing but a thin metal gate] and blow away a bunch of Russians together with the SF guys, Major Kershaw, Bob Mikic, CPT Ans, and me. And the Russians could pretty easily park some heavy vehicles in such a way as to make that pretty difficult, too [but as of 9 Nov 96, when I was there last, they had not].

If there is to be an attack on the Russians and/or Americans at Ugljevik, I don't think it will be by car or truck bomb. Much easier just to lob in a few mortar shells from the other side of the hill.

CPT Ans says it would take 15 minutes or more after firing the first mortar for anyone to get an accurate shot into our camp because of the corrections that would be necessary, by which time everyone would be in a hardened shelter, so unless the first shot was amazingly lucky, they wouldn't get many, or any of us. Back to the car/truck bomb theory.

The Americans stood up the Russians twice in a little over 24 hours this weekend.

A joint Russian-American patrol with 2 BDE was scheduled for Saturday. The Americans cancelled because of the furor over force protection, but neglected to tell the Russians.

A big deal had been made of a get-acquainted trip GEN Casey (GEN Cherrie's replacement) was to make yesterday, arrival being scheduled for 1230. At 1200 they called to say they weren't coming.

HQ 1 AD wants the entrance to every camp in MND(N) (Multi- National Division (North)) blocked by at least one armored vehicle or at least a 5-ton truck. I.e., our three or four Humvees at our front gate wouldn't cut it. We asked the Russians, and they declined to help. Supposedly no American unit could help us, either. So some colonel from TAB was talking to Major Kershaw about it yesterday. The colonel asked, "Do they (the Russians) know it's an ORDER?" "Yes." "Then why aren't they complying?" Answer: a shrug of the shoulders over the telephone, meaning, "And just how do you think you are going to compel the Russians to carry out an American order, especially one they consider terminally stupid?" And since technically the Russians are not under our orders, they can choose which ones to carry out and which ones not. Then Major Kershaw suggested the Serbs might let us have a T-34 tank (a famous WWII Soviet tank the Serbs still use), but the colonel didn't think that was funny. Actually, at the end of the day the Russians did park an Ural 5-tonner at our front gate together with the driver, but I think their front gate is still totally unprotected. [It was.] I do wish they'd block it at night. [The Ural was left at our gate a few days, after which we went back to blocking the gate with several Humvees. By November we were only blocking it with one Humvee, which does seem kind of thin.]

Tues, 13 Aug 96 1730

One of our soldiers accidentally discharged his weapon last night. Fortunately, all he hit was a sandbag. But it has to be officially investigated, etc.

Last Friday GEN Nash informed GEN Gavric that IFOR would inspect VRS facilities in Han Pijesak [pee-yeh-sahk] and on Mount Zep on Saturday at such and such a time. In effect, he was telling him, "Make sure Ratko Mladic isn't there then." But on Saturday the VRS wouldn't let our people in. So a war of nerves was initiated by IFOR, with pressure to be increased gradually until the Serbs crack. Apparently they have, but we don't have official notification yet that the crisis is over.

IFOR encouraged representatives of NGOs (non-governmental organizations) and IOs (international organizations) to pull all their non-local employees out of the RS (Republika Srpska). The RUS BDE helped transport people from the IPTF and perhaps others to Tuzla (not, as I understand it, to TAB). The ICTY people already here stayed. Rebecca ..., from the British NGO "Feed the People," came out from Bijeljina and stayed the night, but decided to return to Bijeljina today.

This morning we spent an hour-and-a-half overflying all the RUS BDE checkpoints and also some other sites in the AOR.

Travel by land has become more difficult because of increased security precautions.

Wed, 14 Aug 96 1200

All the camp dogs disappeared a few days ago.

The Serbs cracked, if that's the right word, and all special measures were cancelled as of midnight last night. The inspections were held yesterday and showed that the Serbs had nothing to hide. So why did they at first refuse to allow the inspections? Probably to rattle our chains and to maintain a state of tension so as to help them keep their own people in line.

When speaking of Serbs, Croats, and Muslims in the former Yugoslavia, it should be kept in mind that in a sense the people as a whole of all three groups have been hijacked, since no truly free and democratic elections have ever to my knowledge been held in this country and certainly not in the last several years. That means power is held basically by those most determined to get and keep it. And even if it should be true, for example, that Karadzic would win freely held elections today, the results would still be tainted because of the near monopoly Karadzic and company have had on information in the Serbian-held parts of Bosnia for several years. And it's pretty much the same everywhere else. Nobody really thinks the elections to be held in September will be free and fair. The hope is that they will be free enough and fair enough to set the stage for following elections to be freer and fairer than these were, and so on.

Which implies continued lengthy and intense international attention and pressure to make it so. Which is pretty problematic. I don't think a less than thuggish regime in the RS is likely any time soon and I don't think the Muslims and Croats will fare much better. The same for Croatia and Serbia proper under Tudjman and Milosevic.

How then to justify the efforts and expenses of the international community in general and ours in particular?

What has been achieved and I think can be maintained is a cessation of large-scale violence and incremental improvements in people's lives and also in political processes. This is a worthy thing by itself.

The alternative: continuing war, poverty, and destabilization in the Balkans with the effects spreading to much of the rest of the Balkans and to Europe and hence to us.

The day-to-day work can be pretty frustrating.

Yesterday RUS BDE CDR COL Generalov organized a meeting to be held at 1000 today at the Russian checkpoint at the IEBL on the road between Lopare in the RS and Celic in the Muslim-Croat Federation between the mayors of Celic and Lopare and between the members of the Lopare LEC (Local Election Commission) and the members of the Celic LEC. Representatives of the IPTF, OSCE (Organization of Security and Cooperation in Europe), and the ECMM were also invited. We showed up, IPTF, OSCE, and ECMM representatives showed up, and so did the Mayor of Lopare and members of the Celic LEC. But the Mayor of Celic sent a deputy and the Lopare LEC didn't show up at all. The Mayor of Lopare refused to talk with the Mayor of Celic's deputy and the Celic LEC had no one to talk to. So it all went down the tubes, primarily because of Serbian obstructionism. Generalov was mad as hell at the Serbs. One Serb I know said his guess is that the local Serbs would have come, but had instructions from above not to.

So even if the Mayor of Lopare would like to represent the true wishes and interests of his constituents, it is not at all clear that he can. This is a guy named Bogdanovic. He spent about an hour with COL Generalov yesterday and agreed to all this, but couldn't deliver. And he may have been glad of the excuse not to meet with the Celic representative. My friend says it's too bad I can't follow what's said on RS TV. Again the issue of information and inflammatory propaganda.

We saw portraits of Karadzic plastered up around Koraj. COL Breslavsky, LNO to the Serbs and Muslims, says they're everywhere. I am sure Karadzic is still pulling all the strings.

131

So all FWPs are carrying out the military provisions of the Dayton Accords, but the Serbs are egregiously violating the agreement on removing indicted war criminals from power and all to a greater or lesser extent are violating freedom of movement and refugee return rights.

1715
COL Generalov's wife and 12-year-old son Dima are visiting here for a week or two. He asked Major Kershaw if he could take his son on the helicopter ride yesterday. Major Kershaw knew he couldn't, but asked the question anyway. The Russians find this sort of thing about us hard to understand. What's the problem? Just take the kid and go. On the other hand, as far as I know, we don't have teenagers in the pilot's seat flying airliners into the ground. Even if we do have small children flying small planes into the ground.

Major Kershaw bought a pair of size small BDUs and had a 1 AD patch and colonel's insignia sewn on them and gave them to Dima.

Dima did get to ride out to Koraj and Celic with us today in a Humvee.

Thurs, 15 Aug 96 0845

Roughly speaking, two thirds or eight months of this one-year mission are over.

On Mon, 10 June I moved temporarily over to the American encampment and finally moved back this last Sunday, 11 Aug 96. I dragged my heels somewhat about going back as in some ways it is more convenient there—in particular the proximity to the American toilet and washing and showering facility and to the American chow hall tent.

My new routine is that I get up at 0640, dress, go to breakfast and the morning news on AFN TV at 0700 in the American chow hall tent, then about 0720 I go wash and shave at the American facility, and by 0745 I am in the office. I read the overnight dump, drink a paper cup of cold cocoa mix, and interpret at the conference call at 0830. After that I do whatever comes up. (I answer the phone a lot—this is nearly always in English.)

This morning about 0815 Major Kershaw was having trouble explaining to the Chief of Staff why four Rumanian soldiers were here, and I helped out. (They were escorting something from Tuzla to Bijeljina and would then return; two of them were American soldiers dressed as Rumanians because somebody thought they would be safer in RS territory that way; all of which sounds odd to me. No wonder the Major needed help.)

Sometimes I go to lunch with the Russians at 1400, but more often I go to the American tent for a couple of little boxes of Rice Krispies or something similar. At 1800 I go to the American tent for supper and the CNN news (American version on AFN TV). After that I drop back by the office and at 1900 watch the Russian evening news program "Vremya," after which I go to my room and/or back to the tent to watch some of our TV, for example "Frasier" on Wednesday at 2000. At 2030 I go to shower in the American facility and from there back to my narrow little room for some reading before bed. Sometimes I get an hour's siesta in the afternoon.

One Russian officer, just back from a couple of weeks in Russia, says things are pretty bad there and that certain events he didn't specify may occur there this fall [they didn't].

Thurs, 15 Aug 96 1030

Several days ago quite explicit orders went out on destroying weapons and ammo confiscated from the FWPs. GENs Nash and Walker wanted to make a big deal of it, with before-and-after pictures, etc. The Russians seized upon the central point: destroying confiscated weapons and ammo. They didn't have very much, anyway—just two AK 47s, two TT pistols, and some ammo to them. So they used a welder to chop the guns up into little pieces and threw the ammo

133

into a water reservoir and drew up a certificate of destruction. But nobody took any pictures and they did the job a day ahead of schedule. So the next day a group of U.S. Army photographers (Combat Camera) came in by helicopter, and we had to scramble to at least get the Russians to bring in the chopped-up guns so they could photograph that.

The Russians, it seems to me, are often like that. They grasp the central point, do it, and the heck with details.

My thumb may or may not be a case in point. Several weeks ago I ripped a piece of skin off my left thumb next to the nail on the left side. Some kind of growth grew up there spreading onto the nail, kind of bead-like. When antiseptic and a band-aid didn't make it go away, I went to the Russian clinic. That was Friday. Two surgeons cut off the growth, sewed up the thumb, and bandaged it. After the anesthetic wore off, it hurt like crazy and I didn't sleep very well, even after taking painkiller our medic gave me. Saturday evening, after getting back from all day at TAB, I went in for rebandaging. The thumb began bleeding pretty copiously. When I went back over to the American encampment, SSGT Aguala noticed the bloody bandage and sent for our medic. The medic had some fibertape-like things he used to pull it up tight and rebandaged it, having stopped the bleeding. So I think the Russians probably did fine on the operation, but the follow-up was faulty, whether through lack of that nifty fibertape-like stuff or lack of attention to detail, I'm not sure. [There is a follow-up to this story: The American medic in a way did me no favor. With the bleeding stopped, I didn't go back to the Russian clinic until the surgeon who had done the operation stopped me on the street several days later and wanted a look. Plus he had expected to see me back in a day or so. When he took the American bandage off, both of us were appalled. The American medic had sealed the wound off from all air and now it was a real mess with something really ugly growing on it. The Russian surgeon was pretty mad. So what if it was bleeding, he said. Nobody ever died of a bleeding thumb and that way the wound stays clean.

Now they might have to do the operation over and in any event he had to cut a bunch of stuff off, which he did without benefit of local anesthetic. Ultimately no further operations were necessary and the thumb is OK. I'm still inclined to think that the thumb shouldn't have been bleeding THAT much, but otherwise the Russian surgeon was right and did a good job.]

1710
We'll be at TAB all day tomorrow and the next day for an election seminar.

Sat, 24 Aug 96 0915

Tues, 20 Aug 96 COL Generalov attended a seminar on the elections scheduled for 14 Sep 96 in Bosnia and Herzegovina.

The day started with a mad rush because once again COL Generalov left in his Uazik without telling us. He must have started with a lead of at least ten minutes, but also once again SGT Carter made real good time in a Humvee unburdened by armor or even a hard top and we caught COL Generalov about a hundred yards from the entrance to TAB. If we hadn't caught him, we would have been held at the gate while Major Kershaw explained why we were traveling in a single vehicle rather than with a convoy. It's a concession at that to consider that one Uazik plus one Humvee comprise a convoy, since when the vehicles are all American ones, it takes four vehicles to make up a convoy.

Today's session ran from 1300 to 2120 with an hour for supper at 1800 plus shorter breaks. The building was hot. A couple hundred people were gathered to hear representatives from the civilian organizations—OSCE, UNHCR, IPTF primarily—talk interminably about the elections followed by an interminable series of presentations by IFOR staff personnel. COL Generalov and I were in the front row and I was more or less keeping up with the first

135

speaker until COL Generalov told me to can it and just give him the highlights of the important stuff. He was bored stiff and got pretty restive toward the end. And he was expected to come up with his own briefing by 1000 Wed, i.e. with no time for preparation.

I think a firm operating principle when operating with the Russians should be that if it's important and goes beyond operations that are immediate (i.e. today and maybe tomorrow), it should be given to the Russians typed out in large thick print in good Russian. Then if you still insist they attend a briefing, at least they and the interpreter have a starting point. This is perfectly do-able if the Americans have one or two competent persons at HQ to do the translations. If it's more than they can do with about a 48-hour lead, then it's more than a Russian commander is going to read, anyway. This would force focusing on the essential. The rest of it is just a deluge of detail that no one person could assimilate, anyway.

The Russians are the only ones who require interpreters, but I'm not sure all the other foreign representatives understand all this as well as is assumed. The Nords probably do, but I have my doubts about the Turks, for example.

And in general the issue of language is given insufficient attention, at least with regard to the Russians. This was true when 3 ID (now 1 ID) was preparing for the joint exercise at Totskoye [TOHT-skuh-yuh] in 1994, it was evidently true at the Fort Polk exercises in 1995, and it's true of this operation.

If I hadn't just wandered onto the scene in Nov 95 and pressed my services on GEN Nash and Major Bushyhead, ALL high-level Russian-English interpreting in MND(N) would be done by Russians, none of whom of those here, as it happens, know English as well as I know Russian. The Russians at their LNO office at TAB perhaps have personnel who could handle the translations I suggested above, but if you want a guarantee the work will get done and to your standards, you have to have your own people.

Considering the millions that are spent on communications, I would think a quarter of a million or so could be allocated to this for an operation of such importance. We are willing to pay millions for what amount to fancy gadgets and the personnel to maintain them, but sometimes not for the brains that would provide content for them to transmit. The Russians at least make substantial efforts because they realize the importance of English, but our foreign-language efforts often seem like the result of afterthought and are usually inadequate.

The American FAO LNOs who work with the Russians and speak Russian to a greater or lesser degree perform essential tasks, and the Russian they do speak is infinitely better than no Russian at all. Having to have an interpreter present for every last little thing would be just unbearable. But by no means all of our FAO LNOs are capable of effective communication. I realize that our FAOs who serve as LNOs are military people first of all, with language being only an enabling tool. I don't pretend to think that I, for example, could handle all aspects of their jobs because I don't know enough about the military. But I still think that greater efforts should be made to ensure that they are capable of expressing themselves effectively in Russian and in understanding what they hear. I would judge effective communication possible for Level 2+ speakers (judged hard-nosedly!!) with Level 2 the absolute minimum. (The first FAO LNO at best was a Level 1 speaker in Nov-Dec 95 and by the end of his time here maybe was approaching Level 2.) If they have tested out at Level 3 in oral and written comprehension, they should with practice be able to make it here in the real world where not all speakers are willing to or are capable of adapting their speech to the needs of foreigners. [The proficiency levels referred to are as defined for the Defense Language Proficiency Test (DLPT).]

A way needs to be found for the military to sustain, improve, and mainly reward the efforts of those officers who have developed their language skills to a reasonably high level and wish to continue. Unfortunately, as it is such people are just as likely, as I understand it, to retard their advancement in the military if they stick to assignments that require their language skills.

Back to reality.

Wed morning we came in for Wednesday's session, but shortly after arrival, COL Generalov learned that a Russian soldier had stolen money within his unit and gone AWOL. It seemed to us that COL Generalov leapt at the chance to skip Wednesday's session; in fact some of us wondered if he hadn't invented it. And in any event in an American brigade the CDR would send his minions to handle the case, rather than heading it up personally.

As it happens they found the AWOL soldier-thief Thursday in a hotel in Belgrade. He had stolen $12,000 from his fellow soldiers and run off, bought a pistol somewhere, and was on the run. They brought him back under armed guard and kept him under guard until they could send him back to Russia. Hard to imagine how he thought he could get away with it.

Major Kershaw had to do COL Generalov's briefing; he says it went all right.

I spent most of Thursday translating MND(N) orders concerning the elections into Russian, the very materials COL Generalov should have had prior to the Tuesday-Wednesday seminars.

Thursday evening five "*kursanty*" just arrived from Russia were settled in the large room to the right as you come into my room. These translations can now be turned over to them.

Yesterday GEN Casey landed at 1100. After a briefing and a walk-around and a private talk with COL Generalov, he, COL Generalov, and I flew over all Russian installations and checkpoints, setting down at one of them to examine it more closely. COL Generalov showed that he did, in fact, have a good grasp of the situation both militarily and with regard to the elections. The day went well, and I think everybody was happy with it. It was the first time I had flown in a helicopter with the side doors wide open, and that was a little startling at first. We flew about 600-1000 feet above the ground. You get a real good feel for the general layout of the area that way.

As to my thumb, it was not, as it turns out, a good idea to totally stop the bleeding and seal it off. The surgeon is pretty disgusted—says now the operation will have to be done over and it will be harder than it was the first time, which was hard enough. It looks pretty gruesome. I'm due back an hour from now.

1430

For three days in a row now, I think it is, they have looked at the thumb, mucked around a little, and bandaged it up again. I have hopes they're not going to operate again. The Chief IFOR surgeon, a COL Tinsley, was here Thursday and I suggested a joint operation, but he wasn't interested. Didn't smile at my pun, either.

Sun, 25 Aug 96 1115

I think the future of Bosnia and Herzegovina looks pretty much like the present, at least for the next several years.

Several days ago I had a look at an analysis by the ICG (International Crisis Group). The ICG wants the elections scheduled for 14 Sep 96 delayed, saying that free and fair elections cannot be held now and that the main result will be to legitimize the power of those who hold it now, none of whom as of now are entirely legitimate. And elections now will legitimize ethnic cleansing and lock in the status quo, whereby ethnic cleansing is pretty well complete all over Bosnia and Herzegovina and is maintained by lack of freedom of movement and return of refugees to their homes, both of which were agreed to by the FWPs in the Dayton Accords, but have not been translated into reality.

The military aspects of the Dayton Accords were tightly specified and have been carried out except for mine clearing, for which the expectations were unrealistic considering the number of mine fields out there and the fact that mine clearing was supposed to be carried out by the FWPs themselves, a task beyond their physical capabilities, especially after demobilization of so many of their soldiers.

But the civilian aspects were not so tightly written and amount more to a set of generally desired results rather than tasks to be accomplished to a schedule. Nor have the necessary resources been devoted to the civilian aspects.

The main point of the negotiations at Dayton, as I see it, was to get the fighting stopped and keep it stopped for at least a year. All sides could agree to that because they all wanted that. But aside from the fact that the immediate purpose of the negotiations was to stop the fighting and keep it stopped, certainly the Bosnian Serbs would never have agreed to provisions in the civilian aspects of the Accords, combined with military enforcement from the military side, which would deny them their victory, that is, the removal of Croats and Muslims from territory under their control and de facto recognition of their entity—Republika Srpska.

I don't see how anybody could have entertained the illusion that the Serbs could be denied their victory short of a full-scale, long-term military occupation by international forces led by the U.S. of all of Bosnia and Herzegovina. And that is just too much to expect of the international community in general and the U.S. in particular. The real goal, as opposed to the stated goal, was to stop the war with its potential for further destabilization in the area, and to stop the further influx of refugees into Europe, and, if possible, to ship many of them back to Bosnia and Herzegovina. That goal does not require the restitching of Bosnia and Herzegovina back together, freedom of movement, return of refugees to their homes, and the establishment of democratic government in Bosnia and Herzegovina. Because the international community [for whatever reason] lacks the will to impose all those good things, and because the will for it is certainly lacking here, it is not to be. The Serbs have won. (Again, I point out that the terms "Serbs," "Muslims," and "Croats" are shorthand for the people who have come to power and who hold power in the various communities and not to the people themselves, since the people themselves have never really been consulted on their desires.)

If the Serbs were the only bad guys out there, I would feel that at the least a terrible crime has been left unpunished. Unfortunately, the Muslims and Croats have done and continue to do a lot to undermine their case.

In 1991 the Muslims under the leadership of Alija Izetbegovic called for the creation in Bosnia and Herzegovina of a state "for Muslims and others." [True, I saw this in a Serbian publication; it bears checking.] This would be like calling for the U.S. to be a state "for white Protestants and others." Such a formulation makes it clear that such a state would consists of two classes of citizens: Muslims and white Protestants, respectively, would be first class citizens and the "others" would be second class citizens. That the "others" might object should not surprise anyone. In particular, the Serbs, comprising about 30% of the population of Bosnia and Herzegovina, objected. And since they had most of the guns and a powerful sponsor next door, they won. The claims of the Muslims that their goal is a secular, multi-national democratic state ring hollow because: 1) they have not given any significant power to non-Muslims in their entity; 2) they are not much better than the Serbs at allowing freedom of movement and return of refugees (or leaving those non-Muslims in peace who tried to stay in the first place); 3) they are dominated by the SDA, Izetbegovic's party, and it is not all that much more tolerant of other claimants to power than Karadzic and his SRS party. [During the centuries of Turkish domination the Muslims in Bosnia and Herzegovina had, in fact, been first class subjects and everyone else second class subjects; in a way Muslim nationalists in Bosnia and Herzegovina seem to be striving to restore the status ante quo.]

141

In brief, the inner resources for free and democratic government do not exist here and the international community's judgment is that the cost of imposing them would be incommensurate with the possible benefit to the international community.

The IFOR leadership surely sees this all pretty clearly and thus resists actions such as hunting down Karadzic and Mladic that would cost casualties and still not guarantee achievement of the political goals of those who call for it.

This is a pretty unhappy country and will remain so until they develop their own internal resources to change it. Which may never happen, and certainly will not happen any time soon.

The good fortune of the Germans and the Japanese after WWII was that the international community led by the U.S. saw clearly that the only way to render them safe to the international community was to impose free, fair, and democratic government on them. Such a convincing case for Bosnia and Herzegovina has not been made. Or for anyone else. (Although there are those for whom it might be made, in particular the Russians [who, fortunately, seem to be coping reasonably well on their own, which is always preferable] [Well, maybe they are and maybe they aren't. Note of 30 May 2004].)

[It turns out the people do share some of the blame. According to Laura Silber and Allan Little in *The Death of Yugoslavia*, (London: Penguin Books, 2nd ed., 1996, p.210), in the elections of late 1990 the overwhelming majority of voters in Bosnia and Herzegovina voted according to ethnicity. Since the Muslims had a plurality, that meant Muslim domination of any government of Bosnia and Herzegovina as a whole, which neither the Serbs nor the Croats, but especially the Serbs, were prepared to accept. There were non- or multi-ethnic parties, but the voters largely ignored them. The people are not always right, either.]

Mon, 26 Aug 96 1100

Somebody at the OSCE seems to have it in for the Russians.

One of the things RUS BDE was mandated to do by directive from Division is to determine whether or not each polling place meets requirements: does each one have at least three windows, have at least X square meters of floor space, etc? RUS BDE found 20 polling places in the Bijeljina *opstina* [op-SHTEE-nah] (municipality or township) that did not meet requirements and so informed Division. In addition, they told the chairman of the Bijeljina *opstina* (or one of his representatives). Someone from the Bijeljina *opstina* apparently told someone at the OSCE that the Russians had cancelled 20 polling places. Someone at OSCE registered a big protest to Division that the RUS BDE is working at cross-purposes to IFOR and OSCE and now Division is in a lather over it. The OSCE has also been in touch with the Russian Ministry of Foreign Affairs with the same complaint. In effect the Russians are being punished for doing what they were told to do plus giving the Bijeljina *opstina* a heads-up that there were problems with some of their polling places. A representative from the Bijeljina field office of the OSCE, Stephen Pern, was here this morning. He was absent when all this happened, but came out as soon as he learned of it to get the facts, upon which he apologized profusely to the Russians. But Division still wants answers in writing. GEN Nash is due out in a couple of hours, and Major Kershaw proposed to CPT McLaughlin at Division that the matter be handled then, to which CPT McLaughlin replied that it wasn't enough to answer to GEN Nash; we also have to answer to the staff at Division. Major Kershaw's theory is that trouble is being fomented by people at Division who are otherwise underemployed, which is partly a result of the 12 hour (or 24 hour) a day seven days a week work ethic at Division HQ. Which also causes them to look down on the Russians, who have a different, and I think more normal, work ethic.

Tues, 27 Aug 96 0940

Bashing the Russians seems to be in style.

Sun, 25 Aug 96, the Central Russian Army (TsSK) handball team was playing the Bosnian Serbs in Doboj [DOH-boy]. That's in the Nordpol (Nordic-Polish) BDE AOR of MND(N). COL Generalov was invited and went, traveling in his Uazik with IFOR markings. He was stopped at three Nordpol checkpoints and showed his ID at each one. Since he had arrived early, he and his small party stopped at a sidewalk cafe in Doboj for a cup of coffee. Nordpol MPs began harassing them, photographing them, and conspicuously tailing them on the way to and at the game. COL Generalov is furious. Apparently the Nordpols declared Doboj off limits to their people, but failed to clear with Division HQ how this was to affect other IFOR elements. At any rate COL Generalov didn't know about it. The Nordpol MPs also wrote up a pretty inflammatory report on the incident.

Some person, supposedly a real "kozel" [kah-ZYOHL] (roughly: asshole), at UNHCR (United Nations High Commission for Refugees) wrote a scathing report alleging that the RUS BDE CDR with the "unlikely" name of Generalov neglected his duty to be at some meeting because he was off meeting his wife in Belgrade. But the RUS BDE has two perfectly competent LNOs, COLs Yevgeny Shamilin and Sergei Breslavsky, who could sit in on such meetings, and the reference to COL Generalov's name was gratuitous and why he was absent shouldn't be relevant.

A week or so ago there was a big commotion about getting ammunition out of Serbian tanks, having it in them being a violation of the Dayton Agreement. The Serbs said they had no other place to store the ammo; CPT Ans personally crawled around those tanks, Soviet-made T-34s (WWII vintage!!) and T-55s and says they are in such bad shape they couldn't possibly be used in combat. GEN Nash did agree to give them a couple of weeks and also to provide wood to build storage racks. I.e. there was nothing to get excited about even though there was a formal violation.

GEN Nash is real keen to get several Russian artillery pieces to do live fire at the Glomoc range. GEN Khalilov replied that they'd love to, but the fact is they can't spare the ammo; i.e. they can't afford to [in the sense that the Army doesn't have the money to buy the ammo]. I.e. if things get hot here, they might not be able to fire more than a few rounds.

SACEUR GEN Joulwan visited Checkpoint 45 in the Russian sector yesterday. That's in the southeast of the Russian sector, over towards Zvornik in 2 BDE's sector. GENs Joulwan and Nash and entourage flew in by helicopter. COL Generalov, Major Kershaw, and I drove overland. Just this side of Priboj we turned left, drove through RUS BDE's 1st Battalion's camp, past the Priboj Reservoir, onto a dirt and gravel road, up and over a mountain, and down past Sapna to Checkpoint 45, a real dusty ride since Major Kershaw and I were not in the lead vehicle. About an hour's ride. This was my first time over that road and only my second visit to Checkpoint 45 (I flew there a week ago with GEN Casey and COL Generalov).

GEN Joulwan was out visiting the troops and passing out memento coins. He pronounced himself entirely satisfied with the way the Russians were dug in. GEN Nash seemed to be enjoying himself, too. CNN and some other media were there.

GEN Nash has tasked me with getting both of us tickets to the ballet the evening we arrive in St. Petersburg, that is, for Fri, 20 Sep 96. I'm trying to delegate that one.

A couple of days ago an American Humvee, part of a convoy operating just a little ways into the RUS sector in the NW, hit an anti-tank mine when the right front wheel went off the pavement while moving over for on-coming traffic. [A member of the crew subsequently wrote to the *Stars and Stripes* to deny that they had driven off the pavement.] The right front of the Humvee got pretty much blown away, but

145

nobody was seriously hurt. The road is one Americans and Russians have been using regularly.

GEN Nash's advice to COL Generalov is that the next time the latter wants to visit the Nordpol sector even informally, he should tell them ahead of time.

Mon, 2 Sep 96 1030

Thurs, 29 Aug 96, was "Let's go to Ugljevik Day."

COL John Batiste, CDR 2nd BDE, arrived at 1000. His visit was cut short about noon when word came of the disturbances in Mahala, in the north part of 2nd BDE's AOR, just south of Dugi Dio in the southern part of RUS BDE's sector. One of the Russian interpreters handled most of COL Batiste's visit.

An OSCE, IPTF, IFOR meeting on security during the election period began a little after noon. I interpreted.

The Army historian dropped by. He wants to talk to soldiers. Chief of Staff LTC Isakhanyan thinks he should talk to several of the key RUS BDE officers rather than just to soldiers.

COL Green of MI dropped by to offer RUS BDE 1 AD EW assets. The Russians somewhat reluctantly accepted them.

There were probably others out here, too, but I don't remember them.

Thursday was the day the Serbs hassled Muslims trying to resettle Mahala, a formerly Muslim village now in Serbian territory. The Muslims were emboldened to do so after 2nd BDE moved its checkpoint in the area east a few kilometers, making the Muslims feel safer in that part of Serbian territory. This area is in the ZOS, where only IFOR and the local police are supposed to have weapons (only handguns for the police). The Serbs brought in 60 or so well-armed policemen from the Ministry of the Interior (the MUPs), (i.e. not the local police). Shots were fired from both sides and several Muslims beaten, one badly enough that he

146

may have died. IFOR arrived and isolated the MUPs and confiscated a number of weapons. Evidently a number of the Muslims were also armed, a clear violation of the Dayton Agreement, and some or most of them may have been military people in civilian clothes. And the Muslim actions were probably not simply those of people trying to return to their homes, but some kind of Muslim manipulations.

Thursday afternoon as an extension of the events in Mahala a crowd in the regional center of Zvornik incited by MUPs attacked the OSCE and IPTF offices in the Hotel Drina. They trashed several IPTF vehicles, dragged a Russian member of the IPTF from his vehicle and held a pistol with a chambered round to his head, and kept all the others surrounded in their hotel for several hours. This Russian in telling about it Friday and yesterday was pretty indignant that IFOR never showed up to rescue them. But eventually things calmed down. See the *Stars and Stripes* for more details.

A meeting was scheduled for 1000 Friday in Zvornik at Zvornik MUP HQ between the Chief of Police there, COL Batiste, and LTC Harriman, and OSCE and IPTF representatives from Zvornik with COL Generalov invited to attend.

Tues, 3 Sep 96 0900

We were late leaving and had to go around by way of Bijeljina, Janja [YAH-nyah] [graffiti with the name "Arkan," one of the bigger war criminals on the Bosnian Serbian side, were up on walls all over Janja and nearby settlements], and down the west side of the River Drina, which forms the border with Serbia proper, to Zvornik. We had our signals mixed, so after a stop at the Hotel Drina, where I took a picture of one of the trashed vehicles, we continued on south of Zvornik when we didn't spot the American vehicles in Zvornik. About half an hour down the road, and already heading west toward Vlasenica, we turned back and this time did spot the American vehicles. It was 1210 when COL Generalov and I finally got into the meeting, which went on another half hour or so.

At times the meeting got a little heated, with the Serbs claiming the Americans always favor the Muslims (if anything, the opposite is true) and LTC Harriman responding hotly that when weapons are pointed at his troops (that had happened Thurs PM), he takes it pretty seriously. It all ended fairly cordially, though.

After the meeting I had a casual talk with a Russian soldier who told me that naturally Russian soldiers want to serve in Bosnia if for no other reason than that they are sure they'll get fed that day, something soldiers serving in Russia apparently cannot count on.

Sunday LTC Soloviev, former Chief of Staff at RUS BDE, who is staying on until after the elections, Major Kershaw, several other Russians, and I flew to COL Batiste's 2nd BDE HQ at Camp Lisa, near Vlasenica. It was a rainy day, and both ways we had to fly way out of our way to avoid mountain passes we would normally fly through and to refuel at TAB.

The meeting there had to do with preparations for the elections. Present besides IFOR were representatives from the OSCE and IPTF and for the second session representatives from the Serbian MUPs and LECs (Local Election Committees).

I have a vague recollection that there was some other meeting Sunday morning at HQ RUS BDE at which I interpreted, but I can't remember what it was.

Yesterday COL Generalov, Major Kershaw, and I flew to Camp McGovern in the 1st BDE AOR for a JMC (Joint Military Commission) meeting presided over by GEN Nash. Muslim GEN Delic, Serbian GEN Gavric, and Croatian GEN Nagulov were there; so were COLs Fontenot and Batiste and many others. Again, it was mainly about election preparations.

GEN Nash is going to be here today.

I am glad to hear that we are punishing Saddam Hussein for his lunge into that Kurdish city. [In retrospect, I am not sure that we did so effectively.]

The word is that GEN Nash will turn over operational control of the American sector in Bosnia to 1 ID (1st Infantry Division) on 1 Dec 96. Somebody from 1 ID called here a couple of days ago, and among other things the topic of interpreters came up. I don't really expect to be asked to stay on after GEN Nash leaves and I have pretty ambivalent feelings about it. I would have to be out NLT 30 June 97. Assuming FLTCE/IES would even approve. And that the Russians stay past January 97.

Before the trip to McGovern yesterday some regional-level OSCE people came in and COL Generalov briefed them on the situation in the RUS BDE AOR.

1620

We met GEN Nash at the RUS BDE 1 BN HQ in Priboj, to where he had driven from TAB and RUS BDE 2 BN HQ at Simin Han. Then we all came on up here and from here GEN Nash flew back to TAB.

GEN Nash's adjutant CPT Carlyle tells me that we are to fly business class from Frankfurt. It's on a Delta flight leaving at 1210 via Warsaw to St. Petersburg.

Wed, 4 Sep 96 1430

We had a call today from HQ 1 ID in Wuerzburg inquiring about our Russian language capabilities. They wanted to know whether my TDY could be extended. I said it was possible and that they should talk to COL Beto at IES at the MC.

COL Generalov came in at 1300 and said our interpreter Slobodan (Bob) has to go—he's been drinking, Generalov said, with Russian officers. Generalov said there are two possibilities: Slobodan can leave alone or he can leave with Major Kershaw. Pretty distressing. [And also likely that with a little time COL Generalov would cool down.]

There are some things the Russians and at least some of the Americans don't see eye to eye on.

GEN Nash is real keen on joint Russo-American patrols not only in the RUS BDE AOR, but also in 1 BDE and 2 BDE AORs. LTC Isakhanyan says the former is OK, but not the latter because RUS BDE can't spare the forces. He says it's like sending your wife to some guy while you go visit a whore. But because GEN Nash wants it, some at HQ 1 AD are pushing for it hard and perhaps are simply afraid to tell GEN Nash why the Russians are resisting.

Lots of people out here today and it's not over yet (at 1530).

There's a tunnel about 1/4 of a mile long on the road between Simin Han and TAB. A day or so ago mines were found under the pavement. No one knows, I guess, why they didn't go off. But if APCs and heavy trucks wouldn't set them off, the Uaziks and Humvees I usually ride in certainly wouldn't.

Thurs, 5 Sep 96 0930

Lots of things going on at once with a certain amount of confusion and irritation. COL Generalov thinks we're watching him too closely, saying Russian brigade commanders have a lot more freedom than their American counterparts seem to have. That may or may not be the case, but we do seem to do more jawing.

We're going to try to save Bob.

I am supposed to go to Priboj in a few minutes with MPs that nobody at our TOC knows anything about.

1015

GEN Casey called this morning to tell COL Generalov that he wants to meet with him tomorrow afternoon. COL Generalov replied that he may not be able to because he's giving a briefing tomorrow at 1130-1200. What Generalov didn't know is that the briefings have been rescheduled for Saturday. Generalov wasn't told because an official order (a FRAGO) hasn't been published yet. I did see the new schedule in writing this morning; why the update wasn't passed on to COL Generalov I don't know.

Fri, 6 Sep 96 0900

I go over to our facilities to shave, shower, and s..., but getting up in the night to p... I do in the barracks and my nose seems to have gotten a lot more critical than it used to be.

Usually these days I arrive at work about 0745 and leave at 1755 to go across the river for supper and CNN at 1800. Sometimes I come back to HQ RUS BDE at 1900 for the news, sometimes I stay at the mess tent for The Simpsons, Frasier, and Star Trek.

Last night half way through Star Trek I was summoned to HQ to interpret and was there an hour.

1100

The picture I am getting is that Bob was a victim of Russian hospitality. The four Russian officers involved are being sent home. We've moved Bob over to our side of the river and I hope we can leave it at that. [Later Bob was transferred to a different American camp.]

It's been cool lately and this morning I put a warm long-sleeve undershirt on over the regular one. The summer on the whole was a lot cooler than I expected. But that seems to have been true in Central Europe, too.

1130

After this is all over, or at least when this phase is over, I think someone should put together everything written about IFOR in the most important Russian publications—*Izvestia*, *Segodnya*, *Nezavisimaya gazeta*, *Moskovskie*

Novosti, Ogonyok, Itogi, maybe *Russkaya mysl'* and a few others—and analyze and/or translate into English. Some of that may already have been done. And I think somebody serious from both sides should try to analyze our experience. The Russians should say, "The Americans do such-and-such," and the Americans should say, "The Russians do such-and-such," the idea being to make future joint operations go better and to minimize misunderstandings. The Russians, for example, think we do far too much staff work.

Tues, 10 Sep 96 0900

Sat, 7 Sep 96, we left early (0815) and spent all day at TAB, "we" being me, Major Kershaw, COS LTC Isakhanyan, and a Russian interpreter, one of the "*kursanty.*" BDE commanders were to brief GEN Nash and each other on their plans for the election period; that took up the morning. In the afternoon a war game was run whereby certain events such as huge crowds gathering with incipient violence were supposed to be beginning and the BDE commanders were supposed to respond. COL Generalov had evaded a similar thing 20 Aug, and he did so again, sending COS LTC Isakhanyan in his place. (Generalov spent the weekend in Belgrade, mainly sightseeing.) LTC Isakhanyan was pretty well prepared and did fine, including on the war game.

The Russians think our planning meetings are far too long and detailed. They expect concisely written orders from above which you are expected to carry out without discussion. That plus poor communications from the bottom up may be what leads them into disasters such as occurred in Grozny (Chechnya) 31 Dec 94—1 Jan 95. [Not all of our people are all that keen on such events as that of Sat, 7 Sep 96, either.]

The VRS invited GEN Nash and his BDE CDRs to meet with them yesterday in Doboj ([DOH-boy] or [dah-BOY] depending on whether you prefer Serbian or Russian pronunciation, respectively) to discuss election issues. A UH-60 Blackhawk was sent to pick up COL Batiste, COL Generalov, COL Fontenot, and polad (political adviser) Felix Vargas in that order and take us to Doboj.

On 1 Sep 96 the IPTF put out a memorandum according to which agreement has been reached that on 14 Sep 96, i.e. on election day, all movement by citizens of Bosnia and Herzegovina across the IEBL and to polling places will be on buses and along designated routes. And in truth the Ministers of Internal Affairs (the national police) of both the Muslim-Croat Federation (or maybe only the Muslims, I'm not sure) and the RS (Republika Srpska) had reached such an agreement. And IFOR, or at least the TFE (Task Force Eagle) part of it, would have been glad to have such an arrangement, but, as the OSCE pointed out, that would be in violation of the freedom of movement clause of the Dayton Agreement. People coming into the RS from the Federation can be encouraged to travel in the buses and along designated voter routes, but not compelled to. As of yesterday morning COL Batiste was of the opinion that the Serbs, mainly in the person of the MUPs, I think, will try to enforce the agreement they think they have, and so when the first civilian car comes across the IEBL we will have our first crisis, and when the first civilian car pulls onto a non-designated route we will have our second crisis. And so it will go. (Muslims attempting to visit their former homes or graveyards or trying to come into the center of towns will also cause problems.)

At the meeting with the VRS, attended on their side by GENs Simic and Gavric, GEN Nash hit that issue hard right from the first and encountered no resistance (except that the Serbs did say that if crowds of thousands of Muslims attempt to flood in, the Serbian people will resist).

On election day there are to be no military activities or soldiers in uniform outside the casernes and garrisons. The VRS have no problems with this; they claim that they, too, favor free and fair elections.

That may or may not be the case, but it's pretty clear that if trouble comes on election day, it will come not from the VRS, but from the MUPs and others.

GENs Nash and Simic were at the head table, under portraits of Radovan Karadzic (unframed, middling-sized) and Ratko Mladic (framed, large). GEN Nash had them make sure no pictures or video was made showing him together with the portraits.

There is (or at least a few days ago was) a poster with Koradzic's portrait near the entrance to HQ 1 BN RUS BDE in Priboj.

The general atmosphere at the meeting was cordial.

Dinner was served after the meeting, but without toasts. It dragged on quite awhile and COL Generalov began getting pretty antsy.

The route back was straight from Doboj to HQ 1 BDE at Camp Kime to Ugljevik and on to HQ 2 BDE at Camp Lisa.

GEN Shalikashvili is to be here tomorrow.

COL Generalov does not know whether a Russian force will remain in Bosnia after Jan 97, but if it does, it will be in brigade rather than battalion size because: 1) for logistical reasons a battalion would be capable of nothing more than sustaining itself, and 2) it is less expensive to maintain a brigade in Bosnia than in Russia, even paying personnel $1000 a month each in dollars. To that I would add that Russia almost certainly will want to remain a player in the game. After what apparently is a defeat in Chechnya, that will be especially important, in my judgment.

Things are hectic and therefore sometimes tense here these days, and Major Kershaw is sometimes sharp with Russians and others. But he doesn't turn hyper or quake in fear. And there is occasional genuine humor. And he doesn't tell lies. I do wish his Russian were better (although it is improving substantially).

GEN Casey always seems to make a special point of being friendly with me. I expect he's that way with everybody, but I still appreciate it.

154

GEN Nash is real excited about the upcoming trip to Russia.

Tuesday afternoon Major Kershaw and I flew over the mass graves site at the Pilica farm near the Drina about due east of here where the ICTY is digging. The belief is that the Serbs executed about 2000 Muslims there. Russian IFOR is providing security at the site. One of our people was there that afternoon. That evening we had spare ribs for supper. The fellow picked one up and said, "Mm, Muslim-91." [Actually, it was Muslim-95, almost certainly one of the men who attempted to escape from Srebrenica.]

Yesterday was Shalikashvili's visit, which was set for 1410-1450 at the new Russian checkpoint just east of Celic on the road to Koraj. About 1000 someone from the JIB (Joint Information Bureau) called and said the schedule had been moved up to 1130. So COL Generalov from here and GEN Khalilov from Vukosavci and the rest of us rushed over there and waited and waited and waited and finally GENs Shalikashvili and Nash and entourage flew in just as scheduled at 1410. GEN Shalikashvili had a good visit and at the end gave a statement that AFN radio has been broadcasting.

More and more at such events either Gena [GYEH-nuh] Kamenev from Vukosavci or one of our "kursanty" or Sergei Oneichuk has been doing the interpreting, which I don't mind—I've done my share.

Back to the mass grave site: originally the ICTY said they would be finished by 13 September. Now they say they won't, and they want RUS BDE to continue guarding them. RUS BDE says they are stretched too thin to do that. The ICTY boss evidently was shouting to Major Kershaw that if they don't, he'll complain to President Clinton and Madeleine Albright. And we are getting mixed signals from Division.

Day before yesterday I spoke briefly to LTC Panzarella. He says it's time to let someone else shine and I can't disagree. So I should be out of here by Christmas.

Elections in Bosnia and Herzegovina took place as scheduled on Sat, 14 Sep 96. On the whole they went all right in the mechanical sense that there weren't any major disorders or irregularities.

RUS BDE did get involved in two controversies.

The agreement between the Celic and Koraj authorities with the Russians as intermediaries was that one busload of Muslim voters at a time would cross the IEBL from Celic to Koraj. But it turned out that many of the voters had not been registered to vote in Koraj, and a lot of time was spent registering them, so much so that close to the end of the day it was apparent that two busloads with 140 people would not have time to complete the process. The solution, agreed upon by both sides, was that these 140 people would return to Celic and vote there, the difference being purely symbolic, since both Celic on the Muslim side of the IEBL and Koraj on the Serb side are part of the same prewar *opstina*. But it looked at first to some as though the Serbs were deliberately preventing Muslims from voting in Koraj.

The second issue was one I got tangentially involved in.

Saturday evening Division called and said there was a report that the Russians had stopped a busload of Muslim voters proceeding from the SE directly to Ugljevik and had made them take the long way around up the west side of the Drina to Bijeljina and thence to Ugljevik. I was the only one in the office at the time, and I ventured the opinion that if the Russians had done that, they had done the right thing because the direct route goes over a mountain with switchbacks in the road and the road is unpaved; a bus might not even be able to make it, whereas the longer route is paved and fairly good road all the way, of which I have personal knowledge since I have traveled both ways. The complaint against the Russians came from some person serving with USAID, a U.S. Government agency. The truth of the matter turned out to be that the Russians were neither

156

here nor there. The RS police had stopped the bus, informed the people that they were traveling on a non-recommended route (all parties had agreed on recommended voter routes ahead of time), and told them, but not ordered them, that they should take the longer route.

In short, the Russians were competent and the Serbs didn't commit any outrages.

It sometimes infuriates the Russians that at least some of us don't seem to trust the Russians to do their job and therefore try to keep a close watch on them.

Sat, 28 Sep 96 0900

A press conference on the Jusici [YOO-see-chee] crisis was scheduled for 1400 yesterday, and since that is in the RUS BDE AOR and has been getting a lot of publicity, COL Generalov left for TAB at 1030. Then the press conference was delayed because GEN Casey and the UNHCR thought they were on the verge of an agreement. But COL Generalov was supposed to meet with the Russian ambassador in Belgrade at 1700, so we left TAB at 1430 not having accomplished much of anything.

Jusici is a ruined Muslim village now located in Serbian territory not far from Dugi Dio and Mahala. It is on strategic ground that the Muslims seem to want to reoccupy as it would then position them to split off the southeastern third of the RS (Zvornik and south) from the rest of the RS. The older people who have returned to Jusici are indeed former inhabitants of the village, but the young men are pretty clearly ABiH in civilian clothes. And the Russians took a bunch of weapons away from them.

COL Generalov asked one old man why they had returned now, in bad weather, rather than last summer, and the old man said, "Because our government told us to." So far it has been possible to persuade the Serbs to merely observe rather than resort to force and violence. Major Tom Haines, presently senior American LNO at HQ RUS BDE

(Major Kershaw is in Jusici) believes the Muslims hope to provoke violence on the part of the Serbs so as to reap PR benefits.

The Marshall Center sponsored a conference on Russo-American military cooperation in St. Petersburg, Russia, 21-23 Sep 96. GENs Nash and Lentsov were among those invited, GEN Lentsov coming from his present assignment as CDR 98th Airborne Assault Division in Ivanovo, Russia. GEN Nash had me included in his party, partly, I think, to reward me, and mainly because he wanted an interpreter at his side at all times. He noted early on that I would probably need to swing by Garmisch to pick up civilian clothes.

The German Air Force flies C-160 cargo planes from Landsberg (just west of Munich) to Zagreb, TAB, and, I think, Sarajevo and back M-W-F, and I was scheduled to fly Wed, 18 Sep 96, spend Thursday the 19th at home, and then fly from Munich to Frankfurt Friday morning, where I would join GEN Nash's party for the flight to St. Petersburg. At breakfast Monday morning Major Kershaw said I should go in to TAB that day as there was no guarantee there would be a convoy to TAB on Tuesday or Wednesday. So I went in Monday morning and was able to get on Monday's flight to Landsberg, where Rosemary came to pick me up. So I had three days at home.

While there I learned that GEN Nash has recommended to MG Meigs, CG 1 ID, which is sending 5,000 soldiers to cover 1 AD's withdrawal from Bosnia in December, and who in fact will probably remain indefinitely, that I stay on for a time until suitable replacement for me can be gotten in and brought up to speed. As of this writing, the target date for me to leave Bosnia is 7 Jan 97.

After three days at home in Garmisch, the morning of Fri, 20 Sep 96, I flew from Munich to Frankfurt and joined GEN Nash's party for the flight to St. Petersburg, Russia, to attend the conference on Russo-American military cooperation sponsored and organized by the Marshall Center. GEN Nash himself came in a little later that afternoon on an American military plane. The conference was held at the Hotel Kochubei [kuh-choo-BYEY] in Pushkin [POOSH-keen] (Tsarskoe selo [TSAHR-skuh-yuh see-LOH]), a few kilometers southwest of St. Petersburg, and ran Saturday-Sunday, 21-22 Sep 96, with Monday for excursions, with the return to Frankfurt and Bad Kreuznach on Tues, 23 Sep 96, and to TAB the next day. Marshall Center Director Dr. Alvin Bernstein was there along with Major Jeff Stimson as his assistant. GEN Nash brought along 1 BDE CDR COL Gregory Fontenot as well as his adjutant CPT Tom Carlyle and me. A raft of American Air Force generals and Navy admirals and other officers and civilians were invited. SACEUR GEN Joulwan came in Sunday for the finale. Russian Deputy Minister of Defense Kokoshin was expected, but couldn't make it, so COL GEN Shevtsov, SACEUR's Deputy for command of the Russian brigade in Bosnia, was the most important Russian present. A number of other Russian generals and other officers were there, the most interesting of whom to us was GEN Aleksandr Lentsov, former CDR of RUS BDE in Bosnia. The hotel and meals were pretty good, but $140 a night for a single room and $50 a day for meals seemed a bit steep to me. [Footed by the American taxpayer.]

Saturday's sessions were devoted to the operation in Bosnia. Everything was expressed in terms of good will. GEN Nash was very generous in presenting me as his interpreter, adviser, and guy who knows all the secrets. One Russian speaker said periodic high-level meetings are all well and good, but there are real problems which crop up during joint operations, for example radio frequencies, and a permanent staff should be set up to deal with them.

Saturday evening GEN Nash dragged GEN Lentsov, who really resisted, and COL Fontenot into St. Petersburg to the Mariinsky [muh-ree-YEEN-skee] Theatre (the Kirov in the Soviet period) to a ballet based on Pushkin's poem "The Fountain of Bakhchisarai." The theater and the ballet were magnificent; I think even Lentsov didn't regret coming.

159

After the ballet, we walked across the street to an Irish Pub (!) for a beer and something to eat. The live music performers were deafening. The sight of Russians in there depressed Lentsov. He told me he hasn't been paid for three months and his soldiers since April. He needs $2.8M to put things right in his division, which for a division is a pittance, but he thinks he has no chance of getting it. I was told even GEN Rodionov, their new Minister of Defense, isn't getting paid (although that may be voluntary). The Russian Army may indeed be on the verge of revolt or disintegration.

On Sunday GEN Nash skipped the morning session, playing hooky in order to tour the Hermitage Museum, for which an English-speaking guide had been engaged privately for him. His special interest was the French Impressionists. We spent about two hours at the Hermitage. After the Hermitage we went to McDonald's for lunch, which was eminently satisfactory. And after McDonald's we stopped at the Cruiser Aurora and even went on board (the shot from the Aurora across the Neva River into the Winter Palace (where the Hermitage Museum is located) signaled the start of the Great October Socialist Revolution on 7 Nov 1917).

In general, all his time in St. Petersburg GEN Nash was like a kid in a candy factory. He had a great time.

The session we missed was on Russian cooperation in our search for American POWs/MIAs in the former Soviet Union. Jim Connell, who has been working on this four years already from the Embassy in Moscow, was a part of this.

A banquet was given that evening at which SACEUR GEN Joulwan was the featured speaker.

Monday morning's excursion was to the Yekaterinsky [yee-kuh-tee-REEN-skee] (Catherine) Palace in Pushkin (Tsarskoe selo). The Catherine in this instance was Catherine I, Peter the Great's widow, and not the much more famous Catherine II (the Great). It has been, or more accurately, still is being fabulously restored from the ruins the Germans left.

Then we had a thrilling ride to St. Petersburg for more touring.

160

The ride was thrilling because we were in a VW van driven by a thin, middle-aged Russian man whose appearance gave no hint at all that in his spare time he is probably a successful race car driver. At one point we were racing down the left of three lanes when suddenly a stopped steamroller loomed in front of us. The driver cut a sharp LEFT and we ended up stopped in the center strip with the steamroller to our right. The van was equipped with a blue light and siren, and we continued on in the same manner.

We were accompanied on all our St. Petersburg adventures by CPT Tom Donovan, who is in his second year at Petersburg University courtesy the U.S. Army. He knows an awful lot about St. Petersburg, certainly enough to impress me and GEN Nash. I believe his language skills are of a high order, too.

Anyway, after being delivered to a place just down the canal from the Church on Spilt Blood (the huge pseudo-ancient Russian church built on the site where Alexander II was assassinated in 1881) where souvenirs, paper mache boxes, etc, were on sale, we went shopping. GEN Nash drives a hard bargain, but bought several boxes. But first we had lunch at a small cafe of the type opening up all over. The local beer, Baltika, is excellent, but the fish soup was less liked. After the shopping spree, we wandered along the canal toward Nevsky Prospekt, on the way GEN Nash buying a picture of the church from the artist. GEN Nash asked the artist whether he paid taxes on his income from the pictures he sold and he said he didn't. That would be typical of everybody who free-lances like that—no record of money paid and received is ever made. And probably no more than a rough guess can be made of such non-reported income. But it has to be quite a lot. For example, free-lance privateer taxi drivers, I would bet, don't pay taxes on their income. Or free-lance repairman, or .... Which has to be part of the reason Russia can't pay its soldiers. From where the artist was we walked past the Russian Museum (this was where I had wanted to go), which I read later is being closed at least temporarily due to lack of funds (I guess that would be like

161

the Metropolitan Museum in NYC closing because nobody would support it). We wandered down Nevsky a ways, had some ice cream, and traveled in two privateer taxis across the river to the Peter and Paul Fortress. We went into Peter and Paul Cathedral, where all the Romanovs beginning with Peter the Great and up through Alexander III are buried (supposedly Nicholas II is to be buried there next year). From there we walked back across the river, through the Summer Garden, and some distance to a cafe where CPT Donovan promised us Russian blini [blee-NEE], thin pancakes which are very good with sour cream and other condiments. Unfortunately, we got there just before 1800, when the cafe was due to close. So we tumbled back out into the street and straggled up to a main drag where CPT Donovan hailed us a regular Volga taxi to go to a steakhouse on Moskovskoe [mah-SKOHF-skuh-yuh] shasse [shah-SEH] (Moscow Highway) out toward Pushkin. GEN Nash sat right front and COL Fontenot, CPT Donovan, CPT Carlyle, and I sat in the back. (I was a little surprised the taxi driver agreed to take us.) Too bad to miss the blini, but Daddy's Steakhouse turned out to be a great place. For less than $30 in the ruble equivalent I had a very tender small steak, big salad, and mug of Baltika beer with service and ambience fully up to western standards. In fact the steakhouse, to judge by language in the menu, seemed to be Finnish.

$30 is a typical week's wages these days in Russia.

From the steakhouse I had to deliver CPT Donovan back to his digs in the center of town and pick up some things, go back to the steakhouse to pick up GEN Nash, COL Fontenot, and CPT Carlyle, and return to Pushkin. Our driver in his '85 Lada (in excellent condition in spite of its 160,000 km (100,000 miles), most of them done in Hungary, true), was a 40-year-old shipbuilder whose shipbuilding is at a standstill, asked 50,000 rubles or less than $10 to take us all the way out to Pushkin. When I proposed paying him $20 nobody objected, although GEN Nash had already spotted me as an easy mark. The shipbuilder was a real nice guy who had been a tank driver and a sergeant in the Army (this interested GEN Nash). He had told me he doesn't regret the demise of Communism in Russia, but times are hard. He voted for Lebed for president.

I can't see that St. Petersburg looks all that different than when I was there last time, in Sep 79, except for the billboards and store signs. But life is a lot different, and, for people who have money, much better. Unfortunately, only about one quarter of the people have money. There are a lot more private cars, although the streets haven't choked up as badly as they are said to have in Moscow. Public manners are evidently still considerably better than in Moscow and in general the city is probably much more livable than Moscow.

Tuesday morning we flew back to Frankfurt. We had VIP treatment through Customs both ways. Pulkovo Airport looked terribly run down compared to what we are used to seeing, although the Departures lounge was pretty good. We flew Delta both ways, the plane both ways being about two thirds full with seats spaced with business-class legroom. From Frankfurt we drove back to Bad Kreuznach, arriving there about noon. Wednesday morning we flew back to TAB.

GEN Nash remarked at one point that FAOs are the wave of the future, are very important, and should be rewarded career-wise.

Sun, 29 Sep 96 0815

Europe went off daylight time this morning, but Russia, which usually changes with Europe, did not. Major Haines had a heck of a time just now convincing the Russians here that they had come to work an hour early; they had to go all the way to the Chief of Staff (the CDR is in Belgrade) to get a decision.

0830

I just now got to page 3 of yesterday's *Stars and Stripes*, which says the time change in Europe has been set

163

back to 27 October. Someone from Division apparently misinformed us and we have misinformed the Russians. Egg on our face! Major Haines at this moment is on the phone talking to someone and doesn't know yet.

0856

No, Bosnia and Herzegovina, Serbia, and France and IFOR in Bosnia and Herzegovina did go off daylight time this morning.

Army jargon run amuck: now we have "frustrated" containers. Major Haines is calling around trying to find out what a "frustrated" container is. This sort of thing is highly frustrating to interpreters and translators. As it happens, Russian has no transitive verb "to frustrate," [well, it kind of does] and therefore "frustrated container," whatever it means, will have to be translated as "container experiencing frustration." From context it is apparent that a "frustrated container" is one with no or inadequate markings on it and no documentation with it. And the Russians probably don't need to know anything about it.

1145

Major Haines has been instructed to call around various areas in the RUS BDE AOR and find out what time they think it is.

Mon, 30 Sep 96 0845

At 0823, but which I thought was 0723, I learned that the time change in IFOR (or maybe it was only within MND(N)) has been rescinded. I had just finished breakfast, but hadn't done my morning ablutions yet. But I had to bust across to HQ for the telephone conference, the ring-around (*obzvon*) for which begins at 0825.

The big deal of the day, as it has been for the past week, is the stand-off at Jusici, where IFOR insists the villagers leave and then return upon completing proper

164

procedures (and presumably unaccompanied by armed young men who are pretty clearly ABiH soldiers).

Tues, 1 Oct 96 0800

It turns out the Federation went on winter time, but the RS did not, and this provides one more excuse for not getting together due to confusion of times. But after 24 hours of confusion, the Federation went back on daylight savings time.

Muslims from Simin Han blocked the tunnel between Simin Han and TAB for a time yesterday to protest the Russian blockade of Jusici. [Some even went over to TAB and protested at the gate there, thinking that TAB was a Russian base.]

We're having some fine early fall weather, but I switched to winter-weight BDUs this morning, anyway.

Major Kershaw just came in from Jusici, where he's been having a great time.

Wed, 2 Oct 96 0915

Yesterday's big news was the crash of a Predator unmanned reconnaissance aircraft about 10 km south of here. The crash site had to be located precisely, proofed for mines, and secured until the crash could be investigated and the debris removed. It will take into sometime today to complete the operation.

GEN Nash met with COL Generalov about 1300 yesterday at CP 34 near Celic and also in Tuzla with Tuzla Canton officials. I would have liked to go and assumed GEN Nash would be expecting me as interpreter, but COL Generalov took his own guy instead (CPT Sergei Oneichuk). Sergei is a fine interpreter and is getting more and more of the action while I get less and less.

An agreement has been reached on the Jusici villages.

There's a report than an elderly Muslim man was killed by machine-gun fire near Teocak.

Thurs, 3 Oct 96 1215

One thing that really makes me angry is that in the nearly nine months that Americans have been stationed at HQ RUS BDE no regular delivery of the *Stars and Stripes* has ever been established. A whole swarm of people just descended on us delivering the week's fuel, etc, but not a single newspaper. Maybe Major Haines will kick some ass. [Major Haines did in fact subsequently sweet-talk somebody into seeing that we got newspapers, and that was effective for a couple of weeks, but when he went down to Jusici and was no longer able to monitor the situation, day to day delivery again became erratic.]

My career here is definitely past its prime. The rest is anti-climax, and if it weren't that GEN Nash recommended that I stay for the transition to 1 ID, I would have been just as glad to return with him. Not that it will likely make much difference in the length of my stay here—a month at the outside, I'd guess.

Fri, 4 Oct 96 1630

It's been very quiet yesterday and today. Maybe the rotten weather has something to do with it.

Sat, 5 Oct 96 0815

My Russian neighbor [the "*kursanty*" were moved out and three Russian doctors moved in], the surgeon who operated on my thumb, spent until 0200 this morning getting something off his chest to his roommate. I didn't feel well yesterday afternoon as it was, so I'm hoping I can spend much of the day today in the office easy chair.

I still haven't seen orders for my current TDY (3 July-15 Dec) except for the paper the MC made up, which is not TDY orders. The hand-off to 1 ID in December is likely to cause confusion, too.

If it weren't for the honor, ..., etc, I'd be just as glad to come home now.

1015

Major Aleksandr Pavlovich Savin collects coins and very much wants a 1995 American metal dollar. He'll trade for a rare Russian or Soviet coin. I didn't even know there was such a coin. How can we find out—maybe on the Internet?

Major Savin is the officer at HQ RUS BDE who would like to be a SCCDE student at the MC sometime.

Fri, 11 Oct 96 1100-1200

There's a minor riot going on right now in Jusici. The inhabitants are mad and are throwing things at IFOR.

Jusici is the mainly wrecked Muslim village in the RUS BDE AOR, the inhabitants of which fled in 1992 and which is now in the ZOS on the Serbian side of the IEBL. Its inhabitants began returning on 20 Sep 96, which they have the right to do according to the Dayton Agreements. The problem, aside from the fact that the Serbs wouldn't be too keen about such a return, was that a suspiciously high proportion of the returning villagers were young men who probably had been and perhaps still were soldiers in the Bosnian Muslim army. Worse, they brought in some weapons with them, a big violation of the Dayton Agreements, and some of which the Russians immediately found.

In brief (for details see the *Stars and Stripes* beginning about 22 Sep 96), a deal was worked whereby the villagers would leave for 72 hours, returning to the Muslim side of the IEBL, and return as each villager established that he or she had indeed been a resident and owned property there. IFOR negotiators were able to persuade the MUPs not to react violently.

That may be ending right now. MUPs have come in with automatic weapons and at least one machine-gun. BIG violations of the Dayton Agreements.

Major Kershaw got into a tussle with a MUP and another pointed a locked and loaded machine-gun at him. [Fortunately, Major Kershaw was unarmed at the moment or he might have pointed and even fired his own weapon (a pistol), and then the fat would really have been in the fire.]

The Muslims are threatening to take five Russian soldiers hostage for every Muslim arrested. Three Muslims were arrested in Jusici by armed MUPs for burning RS flags yesterday. At least theoretically, the Russians should never have allowed such arrests.

There were a bunch of explosions in Dugi Dio early this morning.

The Russians have been getting bad press on Jusici, so they want international organizations to come in ASAP to observe. And they don't want to shoot just become someone is pointing a weapon at them.

Our SF guys are on the way to Jusici. A bunch of our people, headed by Major Kershaw, are already there.

Two F-18s are patrolling overhead. Helicopters are on the way.

1345
A Russian communications van in Jusici is surrounded by an angry mob. All its windows have been smashed.

1530
One of the three Muslims has already been released and the other two will be let go soon.

The phone has been ringing off the hook.

It's a fairly nice fall afternoon.

168

The Muslims supposedly have said that at 1600 they will try to disarm the Russian soldiers in Jusici.

Sat, 12 Oct 96 1430

At TURK BDE in Zenica [zeh-NEE-tsah] they are destroying ordnance the ABiH has brought in. Some mortar shells they brought in make a sloshing sound when moved and have aroused suspicions they contain chemicals rather than explosives. The ABiH don't know, because the shells were captured from the VRS. A chemical officer from HQ MND(N), a Major Miller, was called in and so was the RUS BDE chemical officer, Major Viktor Kudryashov and his assistant, SGT Tonkikh. We were picked up by helicopter about 1700 and landed at Zenica about 1745. We hoped to be in the air again by 1830. But it was nearly a half hour drive to the site where they were destroying ordnance and we were there about half an hour. Major Kudryashov doubted the shells contained chemicals, but because his certainty was only about 99%, the shells will not be destroyed now, but sent away for further analysis.

It was dark by the time we got back to the helicopter and 1930 by the time we took off. Furthermore, the helicopter absolutely had to be back to TAB by 2000, so we went straight there.

Flying down mountain valleys in daylight is interesting enough, but doing so at night, seeing lights and outlines of mountains way above you, is a little spooky. The pilots wear night-vision goggles under such conditions.

We spent the night at TAB and were brought back to Ugljevik this morning by Russian Uazik. Since we left so late yesterday I had a notion we might not make it back and was prepared.

Apparently the Jusici crisis is over. Major Haines has gone down there and Major Kershaw will return here later today.

Now that my room is closed off and ventilation is bad, something, probably dirt in the fiber floor, has given me a bad case of asthma. So I am moving back to a tent on the American side of the river today. I am using something like Primatene Mist which the Russians gave me to control the asthma.

The Jusici business plus their other obligations have stretched the Russians thin. And when we go down to around 5,000 from the present 15,000 or so, we will be stretched thin and so probably will the rest of the IFOR-successor forces. Surely no serious person thinks NATO and its partners here should just leave, because if we all leave, they will be on the brink of war or beyond it here all the time.

Major Haines has determined that the American group at HQ RUS BDE cannot be cut very much if meaningful liaison with the Russians is to continue. A crew of half a dozen or more are required to maintain communications via TACSAT (Tactical Satellite) and the Warlord computer. But these people are American enlisted soldiers, and they have to be provided with force protection, provisioning, and two medics to American standards, none of which the Russians standards correspond to. So that brings the number up to 20 or so, or pretty close to what it is now.

The alternative, I suppose, would be to reduce all the way to one or two LNOs and maybe an interpreter and rely on the Russians for comms, since they do have their own comms. That would certainly give the LNOs and the interpreter a truly Russian, full-immersion Russian experience. In fact it would be much like what Major Bushyhead and I experienced here Jan-Mar, only without American comms or even the capability to patch into them. And that would be so limiting, I doubt it could be seriously contemplated—in effect there would be ONE telephone at American HQ by means of which the LNOs could communicate outside RUS BDE. Well, there is a UN satellite phone system, but it doesn't seem to work very often. And I doubt it's secure. If the requirement for a closed (secure) system were dropped, then I suppose there would be other possibilities. [The small SF group here represents such a possibility, as they have their own communications. That would be OK for a certain amount of voice, but it wouldn't include Warlord, by means of which voluminous printed materials are transmitted.]

The 1 AD pullout will get under way in a big way early in November. 1 AD will remove not just people, but also apparently most of their equipment, with 1 ID bringing in its own. Major Haines doesn't know how that will affect us, since not all the people and equipment here were 1 AD assets to start with.

Mon, 14 Oct 96 0900

Yesterday was a clear and warm fall day; today looks to be the same.

Under SecDef for Policy Walter Slocombe visited the Russian and American camp set up near Jusici yesterday. Major Kershaw and I drove down in a two-Humvee convoy, going down by the Priboj Reservoir and over the mountain (much less dust than in August) and back up the Drina through Janja to Bijeljina and down to Ugljevik.

COL Breslavsky told GEN Nash that he has information that if the Muslims continue their push toward the Drina (and Jusici is less than 10 km from the Drina), thus threatening to cut the RS in two, the Serbs in Zvornik will take action independently of the government in Pale [PAH-leh]. This means there is almost certain to be more trouble in the Jusici-Dugi Dio-Mahala area and very likely violence if not outright military action. It's all very nice for old men and women to return to their homes, and the Serbs evidently will not prevent that as long as it is only in the ZOS [maybe and maybe not: later in one instance the Muslims submitted paperwork ahead of time on 94 homes in the ZOS on the Serbian side of the IEBL with the result that a few days later these homes were blown up in the middle of the night, destroying them beyond all possible repair; the perpetrators have not and surely will not be caught, and it is clear that the Serb authorities connived in this action—see the *Stars and Stripes* for ... Nov 96], but when they are accompanied by armed young men, some of whom have been clearly identified as active duty soldiers and officers in the ABiH and when they are occupying strategic ground to threaten to cut the RS in two, then the Serbs have to be expected to react.

The Dayton Agreements give refugees right of return not just to the ZOS, but everywhere, but I think that is a dead letter. But keeping weapons and especially armed Muslims, Serbs, and Croats out of the ZOS is definitely NOT a dead letter. IFOR has strictly enforced that since the beginning, and if a successor force strong enough to continue to enforce it is not left, then things will get VERY dicey here.

Several houses were blown up last night near Koraj.

1345

Now a Serb crowd is gathering near Jusici and making demands with threats of violence if they are not fulfilled.

1710

I guess they managed to keep things under control.

Mon, 21 Oct 96

Evidently due to the asthma, my resistance was low, and so I caught a cold and have had a bad cough. I'm gradually getting over it, but it takes a long time.

The Serb response to Muslims returning to their villages on the RS side of the IEBL has been to blow up vacant damaged houses.

The Muslims may be blowing some, too, because some of them belonged to Serbs. And a day or so ago a

172

timing device and explosives were found next to a power utility transformer in Koraj.

That and all their wrangling. It takes the patience of Job to deal with these people. An article published recently in the New York Times and reprinted in the "Early Bird" (NYT, 24 Sep 96, p.25, "Hateful Neighbors," by John J. Mearsheimer and Stephan Van Evera) says we would all be better off if we recognized the reality that the Bosnian Serbs, Muslims, and Croats are never again going to live in a unitary state and dealt with the situation taking that as the starting point. I think the American and Russian military here and probably simply all of IFOR has long felt that way, but diplomatic efforts continue to try to force unity. I don't see the point.

The Russians are going to have to let the Chechens go, too, with or without Lebed.

Speaking of whom, with some reservations and fears, I think he is Russia's best hope for the next decade or so. A dangerous one, I recognize. Chernomyrdin and Chubais would probably do fairly well, but until Yeltsin drops definitively out of the picture, there's going to be stalemate and further deterioration. I don't know how much more of that they can take.

Most of all the Russians need a sense of hope and confidence and a feeling that somebody is minding the store. Only Lebed can inspire that.

As Major Kershaw puts it, the dance is about over for me here. For example, COL Generalov is meeting with GEN Nash this afternoon, but he is taking his own interpreter rather than me. Transfer of Authority from 1 AD to 1 ID is on or about 10 November, and my replacement should come in about then, if not earlier. What GEN Nash wanted was for me to cover both the transition to 1 ID and to my replacement. By 1 Dec that should be done and I can go.

We ran out of water on the American side last night, so I'm a little grubby today. We have some extra people here, and yesterday morning I caught one shaving with the water going full blast all the time. Probably there were some leisurely showers, too.

Major Kershaw and I moved into the Warlord/Russian G2 (intel) room yesterday.

Being short of breath is getting tiresome. I'll be glad when this has worked its way out of my system.

Wed, 23 Oct 96 1400

All in all I guess I've been fine. I've joked some that it sure is a good thing I enjoy being depressed. I'm sure I've endured considerably more physical discomfort than in any other single year of my life so far. There were some other strains the first six months or so, too.

Monday at noon Chief of Staff LTC Isakhanyan said I'd be leaving for TAB at 1400 to interpret at a conference there. I was ready to go, although I had doubts about my physical ability to perform—I have bronchitis. Sergei Oneichuk, who does most of COL Generalov's interpreting now, was also ready to go. At 1445 (maybe a bit earlier) COL Generalov told us we wouldn't be going. The reason was that there wasn't room in his vehicle (he's using a Niva these days and three's a crowd in the back—a Uazik has space for one behind the rear seat). At 1530 CPT McLaughlin called from TAB to say that GEN Nash wanted to know where the hell Jim Nelson was. At 1535 Chief of Staff COL Brown called to say the same thing. I took both calls. It turns out GEN Nash had given explicit instructions that I was to come.

If we had known that, we would have laid on a Humvee to follow COL Generalov. The conference went four hours and Gena Kamenev (from the Vukosavci group) had to do it all.

A week ago Monday I developed a severe head cold—I think my resistance was low from the asthma. About Wednesday I started coughing. I've been taking Robitussin, which helps some, and I've been getting gradually better. But

I may have some heavy stuff coming up: GEN Abizaid, GEN Casey's replacement, on Friday and GEN Meigs on Saturday. I may or may not be in very good shape and if I'm not, I'll need to be able to say I sought help, so I went to the Russians today. I did some steam breathing, they gave me some pills, told me to drink water with soda, and this evening will put a mustard plaster on me.

Major Bushyhead kept our quarters at about 90 F all the time. Now they insist on two kerosene space heaters in our tent, which keeps it at about 90 F plus oxygen must be down to about 5%. Fortunately my cot is next to the door flap at our end, so I keep that open.

And last night I stormed into the mess hall tent next door at 2200 and turned the TV down to about 120 decibels.

1730

Major Kershaw kept going round and round with Major Lunev, the Russian intel guy, about some 303rd BDE (VRS). Major Lunev said several times, "*Nyet takoy brigady*." (There is no such brigade.) Eventually I realized that Major Kershaw simply didn't understand and I simply couldn't imagine that he didn't understand. [It wasn't because his Russian isn't good enough; he was probably just fixated on something else.] When I finally said, "John, there ain't no such brigade," he said, in effect, "Well, why didn't you say so?" and everything fell in place. Practically the only useful thing I've done all day. But without my prompt, the misunderstanding was total.

Thurs, 24 Oct 96. 0815

No time to write. Getting on a helicopter at 0930.

Mon, 28 Oct 96 1030

A delegation from GEN Shevtsov's office at SHAPE was visiting the area last week, specifically COL Prokudin and LTC Gil Villahermosa. Thursday morning we flew by helicopter to Jusici to show the scene to GEN Shevtsov's envoys.

The Russian in charge on the helicopter, COL Yatsenyuk, wanted to set down at an LZ above Jusici, but the LZ was unsecured, some locals were standing around, and an unidentified vehicle was approaching. The helicopter pilot refused to land, which COL Yatsenyuk thought was being excessively cautious. So we sat down at an LZ that was secured and where in fact we were expected. From there we rode on top of a Russian BTR (APC) first to the American camp, where Major Haines is in charge, and then on to a Russian checkpoint about a kilometer from Jusici itself. It was a cold and damp morning, and it was clear that "'twas the season to be muddy." LTC Villahermosa had me stay at the checkpoint, perhaps because he was aware that I was only marginally physically fit for duty, while the rest of the party tramped on to Jusici, where they had a meeting with the mayor. LTC Villahermosa is big on safety and observing all the regulations and made me wear my Kevlar helmet and flak jacket. I turned out to be glad for the flak jacket because of the cold, but the helmet was a drag.

1230
While waiting at the checkpoint, I talked some with the Russian soldiers there. They have a lot to be dissatisfied about: conditions in Russia continue to deteriorate, their president is an invalid, they don't really get treated right by all their officers [although they were telling me about this in the presence of one of their officers], and their living conditions are pretty primitive and not well equipped. As to Lebed, one soldier said Lebed had simply been deceived: Yeltsin got his support for the presidential elections by giving him an important job, but after Yeltsin won, Lebed became expendable.

LTC Villahermosa says the Russians at SHAPE are poorer than anybody in NATO, including the Turks. Each gets an allowance of $1000 a month, and it's not nearly enough. So Russian officers dread being assigned there, even though things at home aren't very good, either.

One soldier mentioned, for example, that the widows of officers killed in Chechnya aren't even being paid the compensation to which they are entitled, and to call that a disgrace is to put it mildly.

Nothing the soldiers said was new to me, but it was interesting to hear them say it.

We were supposed to be on the ground at Jusici an hour, but we were there two hours, after which we returned to Ugljevik.

1 ID CG MG Montgomery Meigs, accompanied by my replacement, CPT Robert Protosevich, came out to meet COL Generalov Saturday. They had a good meeting. GEN Meigs is lower-key and less flamboyant than GEN Nash. His big enthusiasm is hunting.

CPT Protosevich came out to Ugljevik to stay yesterday. His Russian isn't as good as mine, but it's pretty good and he will do fine. Since he's military, his functions will be broader than mine, anyway. He expects to be here for just one six-month's TDY from the Marshall Center. Unlike me, he did not request the assignment [but he has a positive attitude toward it].

Mr. Yury Baturin, Secretary of the Russian Defense Council, is visiting the former Yugoslavia, and GEN Nash flew out this morning to meet with him. Everybody professed themselves totally satisfied with everyone else. GEN Staskov is a member of the visiting group and greeted me cordially.

I learned yesterday afternoon that I will be leaving Bosnia 10 Nov 96, the day of TOA from 1 AD to 1 ID. My understanding is that I am to fly out on the same plane as GEN Nash, the same way I came in.

Mr. Baturin and party are flying to Pale in an American helicopter to meet with Momcilo Krajisnik, the Serb member of the three-member presidency of Bosnia and Herzegovina. The Muslim and Croat members, Alija Izetbegovic and Kresimir Zubak, respectively, indicated they were too busy to meet with him. So much the worse for them.

As GEN Nash pointed out again today, if the Bosnian Muslims think they are more important to the U.S. than Russia is, they are making a big mistake. Russia and the U.S. are in this together, and the Muslims will not be able to drive a wedge between us. And the Serbs are beginning to realize that the Russians won't do them any special favors, either.

Sat, 2 Nov 96 1050

We had some excitement yesterday.

Day before yesterday a UNHCR vehicle hit a mine on a dirt road a little to the east of Teocak. No great damage was done, but GEN Nash asked the Russians to proof the roads in the area for mines. At one point there is a T-intersection with the top of the T being in Serbian hands, but the vertical member of the T leads to an area Muslims are resettling. Russian engineers proofed the right track of the road as you descend the T, crossed over, and were coming back up when one of the group of seven stumbled. As he stumbled, his left foot went into the center of the road and struck an anti-personnel mine. As he fell backward either his body or his left hand struck another mine and then either his body or his hand struck still a third mine. This was at approximately 0830 yesterday morning.

At 0905 the Russians told us one of their soldiers was sick or injured and that they wanted us to get a medevac helicopter out here ASAP in case medevac to American facilities proved necessary. Two helicopters came in about 0930. I went over to the Russian medical point, getting there just as the soldier was being lifted off the BTR (APC) on top of which he had been brought in. He made some noise as he was jerked about. I could see that his left foot was twisted grotesquely.

The other six members of the group had greater or lesser injuries from flying debris and mine fragments. The

178

face of one in particular was marked up and his left eye was swollen shut. They all looked pretty shaken.

By about 1000 there was a decision to operate on the first soldier here, but to take the two soldiers with eye injuries to the new American facilities at the so-called Blue Hospital. From there soon came the request to the Russians for permission to take them to a French-German hospital near Split, Croatia (on the coast), where facilities are better, and subsequently one of them was taken to Ulm, in Germany, as otherwise they did not think they could save his eye.

The Russian surgeons here amputated the first soldier's left leg below the knee and his left arm below the elbow. On Monday we will medevac him by air to Belgrade, from where he will be taken to Russia on a commercial Aeroflot flight.

The soldier who lost body parts is a Junior Sergeant. His future probably isn't very bright. Russian prosthetic devices haven't been up to our standards [they may be better now] and the disability pension he will have coming, assuming even that it is paid, will probably not be enough to live on even minimally.

CPT Protosevich thinks that the mines on that road were placed there recently by Muslims as a way of keeping Serbs from coming down that road.

So a handful of politicians set all this in motion, but the price in blood, pain, and blighted lives is paid by people like a young Russian no one has ever heard of. I hope Milosevic, Karadzic, Mladic, Tudjman, and maybe Izetbegovic rot in hell forever.

Yesterday afternoon I flew with COL Sergei Breslavsky, Deputy Brigade CDR, to Camp McGovern, SW of Brcko, to the last JMC session to be chaired by GEN Nash. High-level Serbian, Croatian, and Muslim military personnel attended as did the leading lights from MND(N) and 1 ID, including GEN Meigs. It amounted to GEN Nash's farewell to them and the passing of the torch to 1 ID.

179

On Thursday MND(N) conducted a house-to-house search for weapons in Jusici. No weapons were found and GEN Nash pronounced the operation a big success. But there is a different view on that.

On Tuesday COL Breslavsky proposed that the operation be conducted on Friday and furthermore that care be taken to prevent the Muslims in Jusici from learning about it ahead of time, in which case weapons would almost certainly be found.

Yesterday (Friday), after our return from Camp McGovern, I asked COL Breslavsky whether he was satisfied with the outcome of the search. He said it had been a failure in two respects: first of all because the Serbian police had not participated even though they were invited to do so, and secondly because since word got out and no weapons were found, the Serbs are even more convinced than before that both the Russians and the Americans favor the Muslims. I asked whether COL Breslavsky's plan had even been made known to GEN Nash and he said he believed it had, but that for his own reasons GEN Nash had achieved exactly what he wanted: the chance to announce that there were no weapons in Jusici.

GEN Nash has had trouble connecting with RUS BDE CDR COL Generalov on Jusici the past couple of weeks, and I know that this has troubled him. I'm not quite sure where the disconnect it, except that I do know that COL Generalov has not wanted Russian soldiers going into houses to search for weapons—that's police business, he says—and in fact he has given orders that they will not do so. That in part, at least, is why Americans and others participated in Thursday's operation.

That brings us back to the problem of effective communication with the Russians.

I'm linguistically qualified, but for a lot of this I'm not professionally qualified. Besides that, perhaps in part because Major Bushyhead had trained me that way, I have tended to interpret my mandate narrowly. That is, I haven't tended to strike up private conversations on topics having to do with current operations.

Yesterday was an exception, but I had had the feeling that COL Breslavsky hadn't been heard out and I thought talking to me at least might mollify him to some extent.

The ideal Chief LNO would be someone whose Russian is as good as mine and who is as professionally qualified as Majors Bushyhead, Wilhelm, Kershaw, Haines, Choppa, Stimson, or Cecil or CPTs McLaughlin, Ans, and Protosevich. There probably aren't any such people [CPT Protosevich is a reasonable approximation, though], and I don't think it would be wise to lower the professional standards. I would suggest aiming for a speaking standard of Level three by DLPT criteria and setting the Listening and Reading standard at Level three minimum.

And an effective LNO has to be temperamentally qualified, and that's the trickiest thing of all.

My suggestion for the future is that the Army try to identify a pool of officers within its ranks who possess the requisite linguistic, professional, and temperamental qualifications for Chief LNO (I think they might not find more than a half a dozen or so in the entire Army), track them, and when the need arises, as it did late last year, rapidly slot one of them into the position rather than simply going with what you've got, as they did then. Given the overwhelming importance of the success of Russo-American relations, as GEN Nash has recognized from the very beginning, this surely is do-able. And I repeat and emphasize, professional qualifications (and temperamental ones, too) are more important than linguistic ones; if anything has to be sacrificed, it is the latter. [An alternative scheme might be to require top-notch (defined as Level three) language capabilities not from the Chief LNO, but from at least one of the other LNOs serving with the Russians; for this to be effective there would have to be good interpersonal relations between that LNO and the Chief LNO, as the perception could form that the LNO with the better language capabilities was "in thick" with the Russians.]

On an operation of this scale, there should also be a slot for a highly qualified interpreter on the American side. The interpreter should be Level five in all skills in English and at least Level four in all skills in Russian, that is, a person of roughly my language skills.

None of the Russian interpreters involved on a day to day basis with the mission in Bosnia, good as they are, has been better than Level two plus in English speaking skills and perhaps Level three in aural comprehension skills. Their English speech tends to be stiff and stilted, which perhaps is not a fatal defect, but their knowledge of English is not good enough to catch the colloquialisms so frequent in American speech and sometimes they miss quite a lot, especially in informal circumstances. Anyone can learn terminology on demand; it is the overall high-level grasp of a language that is so much more difficult. So if the American interpreter possesses Level four Russian, he or she can compensate for the weaknesses of the Russian interpreters.

Naturally, it would be nice if at least one of the Russian interpreters possessed Level four skills in English, but evidently it is pretty hard if not impossible to get them to go out into the field with the Army (I'm not sure, for that matter, that there is more than one American anywhere to be found who has Level four skills in Russian and is willing to go into the field, and his tour is coming to an end).

[A rough description of DLPT (Defense Language Proficiency Test) skill levels in speaking would be about as follows:

Level five is the level of a highly educated native speaker;

Level four, with reference to a speaker for whom the target language is not native, is the level of a person who has close to 100% control of the structures of the target language and whose speech sounds natural rather than stilted, although there may be a noticeable accent. Such a speaker possesses a broad and deep vocabulary and in ordinary speech uses words and phrases which sound entirely natural to native speakers. Nevertheless such a speaker's vocabulary will be deficient in many areas of interest; the total volume of the knowledge of the target language by a Level four speaker is perhaps one half that of a Level five speaker.

Level three is the level at which a speaker for whom the target language is not native does not make systematically noticeable structural errors and whose vocabulary is broad and deep enough to allow him or her to converse fairly fluently in most areas of interest. The accent of such a speaker is not bad enough to seriously hinder other people's comprehension of what he or she is saying. Such a speaker can express himself or herself fairly effectively, but his or her speech, his or her accent aside, is clearly foreign and many of the words and phrases in such a person's speech reflect "near misses," rather than what a native speaker would have been likely to use in the same context. The total volume of the knowledge of the target language by a Level three speaker is probably considerably less than half that of a Level four speaker. Only a small minority of American students of Russian ever achieve Level three speaking.

Level two speech is the level at which a speaker either has the structures pretty well under control or has a fairly extensive vocabulary, but not both. His or her accent may or may not be perceived as terrible by native speakers and his or her speech is not fluent. The total volume of the knowledge of the target language by a Level two speaker is probably not more than half that of a Level three speaker. It is sufficient for routine day-to-day business, but not for discussion of any topic in any kind of depth. Level two is the level which may reasonably be expected of the better graduates of the Basic 57-week Russian course at DLI (the Defense Language Institute). In my judgment, about half the LNOs of my acquaintance speak Russian at Level two, about a third speak at less than Level two, and the remainder are better than Level two.

The "plus" levels reflect proficiency at about 75 to 85% of that of the next higher level. There are no precise boundaries between the levels.]

Mon, 4 Nov 96 0800

Yesterday morning somebody a km or so away fired a long burst of automatic weapons fire, followed by a shorter burst. Probably celebrating.

At 0030 this morning there was an explosion nearby that sounded like a sharp crack of lightning. The Russians don't appear concerned and Major Kershaw thinks it might have been a transformer blowing.

There have been a lot of 1 ID people out here, some of them staying. And 1 AD people have begun moving out. Only SSGT Adams and I are left of the people who came out here 14 Jan. He leaves a week or so after I do.

TAB
Mon, 11 Nov 96 0930

The explosion we heard the other night was the mayor of Ugljevik's car being blown up.

COL Generalov learned to his dismay last Tuesday or Wednesday that the brigade he also commands near Tula is being turned over to the infantry and he thereby loses status to command the RUS BDE in Bosnia, which is part of the Airborne, and that he is to return to Russia to an unknown future today. He may even have to leave the Army. He is pretty upset. He does have some slight hope of reinstatement as RUS BDE CDR and he says it might help if SACEUR GEN Joulwan were to put in a word for him. I reported that to GENs Nash and Meigs.

I left Ugljevik Saturday evening to accompany COL Generalov to a farewell dinner GEN Nash had with his BDE CDRs and just stayed at TAB after the dinner. I am to leave Bosnia this afternoon on a German C-160 for Landsberg.

Thursday I will drive to Bad Kreuznach to turn in my issue (Kevlar helmet, flak jacket, sleeping bag, etc) and to do some paperwork.

I'm a stranger at TAB now and I feel kind of discombobulated.

Yesterday at the PX I bought a book titled *The Death of Yugoslavia* by Laura Silber and Allan Little (London: Penguin Books, 2nd ed., 1996). Very interesting.

Garmisch-Partenkirchen, Germany
Fri, 6 Dec 96 1345

I flew to Landsberg the afternoon and evening of Monday, 11 Nov 96 and drove to Bad Kreuznach Thursday, returning Friday. I have spent my time since my return putting this journal into shape.

I always had faith that when this was over I would be glad that I had done it, and I am. I believe that by and large we are doing the right thing in Bosnia, and most of all I believe that we are doing the right thing in forging links of military cooperation with the Russians. I am proud that I was able to make some small contribution to these endeavors and I am grateful to GEN Nash and Major Bushyhead at 1 AD for taking me to Bosnia with them and to Major Squires, COL Beto, and Dr. Bernstein at the Marshall Center for letting me go.

James Nelson

Alphabetical list of abbreviations used
in the journal

AB: Air Base
ABIH: Armija Bosnii i Herzegovine; the Army of Bosnia and Herzegovina
AD: Armored Division; 1 AD: 1st Armored Division, United States Army
AFN: Armed Forces Network; television and radio for people in or associated with the American military overseas
ammo: ammunition
AOR: Area of Responsibility
APC: armored personnel carrier
Apr: April
ARRC: Allied Rapid Reaction Corps
Aug: August
AWOL: Absent Without Leave
BDE: brigade
BDU: battle dress uniform, the camouflage uniform worn by soldiers in the field
BG: Brigadier General
BiH: Bosnija i Herzegovina; Bosnia and Herzegovina
BN: battalion
BTR: bronetransporter [bruh-nyeh-truhns-pahr-TYOR]; Russian (or Soviet) armored personnel carrier
C: Celsius
CDR: commander
CG: Commanding General
COL: Colonel
COMARRC: Commander, Allied Rapid Reaction Corps; NATO Commander of Ground Forces in Bosnia
COMEAGLE: Commander, Task Force Eagle (1 AD in the field on this mission), i.e. GEN Nash
comms: communications
COS: Chief of Staff
CP: Checkpoint
CPT: Captain
CWI: Chief Warrant Officer One
CWO: Chief Warrant Officer
DAC: Department of the Army civilian
DB: decibel

187

Dec: December
DM: Deutschmark; a dollar is worth about one and a half Deutschmarks
ECMM: European Community Military Monitors
EW: electronic warfare
F: Fahrenheit
FAO: Foreign Area Officer; an officer specializing in some foreign country or area
Feb: February
FLTCE: Foreign Language Training Center Europe
FOM: Freedom of Movement
FRAGO: Fragmentary Order; I think only the military comprehend what a FRAGO is
Fri: Friday
FWP: former warring party
GAO: General Accounting Office; Congress's watchdog agency
GEN: General
hrs: hours
HQ: headquarters
ICTY: International Court Tribunal for the former Yugoslavia
ID: Infantry Division; 1 ID: 1st Infantry Division, United States Army
IEBL: Inter-Entity Boundary Line
IES: Institute for Eurasian Studies; a division of the Marshall Center
IFOR: Implementation Forces; the forces designated to enforce the Dayton Peace Agreement
IPTF: International Police Task Force
LZ: Landing zone
Jan: January
JIB: Joint Information Bureau
JMC: Joint Military Commission; a meeting of high-ranking officers and sometimes others from IFOR and the FWPs
Jul: July
Jun: June
LEC: Local Election Committee
LG: Lieutenant General
LNO: Liaison Officer
LTC: Lieutenant Colonel
Mar: March
MASH: Mobile Army Surgical Hospital
MC: Marshall Center
medevac: medical evacuation
MG: Major General
MI: Military Intelligence
MND(N): Multi-National Division North; formed around 1 AD
Mon: Monday
MRE: Meals, Ready to Eat, the current U.S. Army dry ration

MUP: Serbian, Croatian, or Muslim Ministry of the Interior; the national police
NLT: not later than
NORDPOL: Nordic-Polish
Nov: November
NTV: Nezavisimoe televidenie; Independent (Russian) Television
NW: northwest
Oct: October
ORT: Obshchestvennoe rossijskoe televidenie; Public Russian (1st Channel) Television
OSCE: Organization for Security and Cooperation in Europe
OSIA: On-Site Inspection Agency
polad: political adviser
PX: Post Exchange; a store for people in or associated with the military
recon: reconnaissance
RS: Republika Srpska; the (Bosnian) Serbian Republic
RTV: Rossijskoe televidenie; Russian (2nd Channel) Television
RUS: Russian
RUS BDE: Russian Brigade
R&R: Rest and Recreation
SACEUR: Supreme Allied Commander, Europe; the chief NATO military commander
Sat: Saturday
SecDef: Secretary of Defense
Sep: September
SF: Special Forces
SFC: Sergeant First Class
SGT: Sergeant
SSGT: Staff Sergeant
Sun: Sunday
SW: southwest
S&S: *Stars and Stripes*, a newspaper published for people in or associated with the American military overseas
TAB: Tuzla Air Base
TACSAT: Tactical Satellite
TDY: Temporary Duty
TFE: Task Force Eagle; 1 AD in the field for this mission
Thurs: Thursday
TOC: Tactical Operations Center
Tues: Tuesday
UN: United Nations
UNHCR: United Nations High Commission for Refugees
V: volt
VRS: Vojska Republike Srpske [VOY-skah] [re-POOB-lee-keh] [SRP-skeh]; Army of the Republika Srpska

Wed: Wednesday
WWI: World War I
WWII: World War II
XO: Executive Officer; Chief of Staff at the battalion or brigade level
ZOS: Zone of Separation

Place Names Pronunciation Guide

Banja Luka: [BAH-nyah] [LOO-kah]
Bijeljina: [bee-yeh-LEE-nah
Brcko: [BRCH-ko] ("BRCH" as in "birch")
Celic: [CHEH-leech]
Chechnya: [cheech-NYAH]
Doboj: [DOH-boy].
Dushanbe: [doo-shahn-BEH]
Han Pijesak: [pee-YEH-sahk]
Janja: [YAH-nyah]
Jusici: [YOO-see-chee]
Koraj: [KOH-rai] ("rai" as in "rye")
Lopare [loh-PAH-reh]
Lukavac: [LOO-kah-vahts]
Pale: [PAH-leh]
Priboj: [PREE-boy]
Pushkin: [POOSH-keen] (Tsarskoe selo [TSAHR-skuh-yuh
see-LOH])
Sarajevo: [sah-rah-YEY-vo]
Teocak: [TEH-o-chahk]
Ugljevik [OOG-lyeh-veek]
Vlasenica: [VLAH-seh-nee-tsuh]
Vukosavci: [voo-ko-SAHF-tsee]
Zenica: [zeh-NEE-tsah]

Index of Names and Pronunciation Guide
to Names

Jarotsky, Alexander, CPT [yih-ROHT-skee]—100
Johnson, David, SSGT—10
Joulwan, George, GEN—24, 31, 32, 33, 43, 60, 76, 97, 98, 107, 113, 145, 159, 160, 184
Kamenev, Gennadii, CPT [KAH-mee-nyif], [gyeh-NAH-dee]—71, 155, 174
Kamenir, Victor, SSGT—115
Kane, Ed, LTC (later COL)—65, 101
Karadzic, Radovan [kah-RAH-jeech], [RAH-doh-vahn]—109, 112, 113, 125, 130, 131, 141, 142, 154, 179
Kazan, Elia—74
Kelso, ..., PVT—125
Kershaw, John, Major—104, 105, 107, 110, 113, 115, 121, 122, 124, 125, 128, 132, 133, 135, 138, 143, 145, 148, 149, 152, 154, 155, 158, 165, 168, 169, 171, 173, 174, 175, 181, 184
Khalilov, ..., GEN [khah-LEE-luf]—110, 113, 124, 145, 155
King, B.B.—115
Kokoshin, A.A. [kah-KOH-shin]—159
Krajisnik, Momcilo [krah-yeesh-neek], [mohm-chee-lo]—177
Kudryashov, Viktor, Major [kood-rih-SHOHF]—169
Lebed, Aleksandr [LYEH-bit], [ah-leek-SAHNDR]—2, 3, 99, 100, 106, 111, 163, 173, 176
Lentsov, Aleksandr Ivanovich., COL (later GEN) [leen-TSOHF], [ah-leek-SAHNDR] [ee-VAH-nuh-veech]—1, 2, 3, 4, 17, 20, 25, 27, 29, 31, 33, 34, 35, 36, 38, 39, 40, 41, 42, 43, 44, 46, 47, 48, 49, 50, 51, 53, 54, 55, 56, 57, 58, 59, 60, 62, 63, 64, 66, 67, 68, 69, 70, 71, 77, 78, 79, 80, 82, 84, 85, 88, 91, 92, 93, 94, 96, 97, 98, 99, 100, 101, 102, 103, 104, 106, 107, 108, 109, 110, 111, 112, 113, 114, 119, 125, 158, 159, 160
Lentsova, Marina—85, 88, 91, 90, 92, 93, 94
Little, Allan—77, 142, 185
Ljubojevic, Dragomir [lyoo-boh-YEH-veech], [DRAH-go-meer]—125
Lodall, Jan—102
Lorenz, ..., Major—3, 5, 6, 7, 8, 15
Lunev, ..., Major [loo-NYOHF]—175
Malkic, ..., GEN [MAHL-keech]—85, 88
Markovic, Slobodan [MAR-ko-veech], [SLOH-bo-dahn]—96, 97
McLaughlin, Chuck, CPT—126, 143, 174, 181
Meigs, Montgomery C., MG—158, 175, 177, 179, 184
Mearsheimer, John J.—173
Mikic, Slobodan (Bob) —[MEE-keech] 124, 127, 149, 150, 151
Miller, ..., Major—169
Milosevic, Slobodan [mee-LOH-sheh-veech], [SLOH-bo-dahn]—12, 130, 179
Mladic, Ratko [MLAH-deech], [RAHT-ko]—10, 53, 109, 112, 113, 129, 142, 154, 179

Morton, Bob—50

Nagulov, ..., GEN [nah-GOO-lof]—148

Nash, William L., MG—1, 2, 3, 7, 11, 12, 15, 20, 21, 22, 25, 27, 28, 29, 30, 31, 32, 33, 34, 36, 37, 38, 39, 40, 41, 44, 45, 46, 49, 50, 51, 53, 55, 57, 60, 62, 63, 66, 68, 69, 71, 75, 76, 79, 82, 83, 84, 85, 86, 87, 88, 91, 93, 94, 95, 96, 97, 98, 99, 102, 103, 104, 106, 107, 110, 111, 112, 113, 114, 115, 116, 119, 121, 122, 124, 125, 126, 129, 133, 136, 143, 144, 145, 146, 148, 149, 150, 152, 153, 154, 155, 158, 159, 160, 161, 162, 163, 165, 166, 171, 173, 174, 177, 178, 179, 180, 181, 184, 185

Nelson, Emily—18, 19

Nelson, Nika—19, 39, 67, 73, 108, 115

Nelson, Rosemary—23, 24, 72, 73, 74, 158

Nevzorov, Aleksandr [nee-VZOH-ruf], [ah-leek-SAHNDR]—99, 100

Oglesby, Dennis, CW1—100, 105, 103

O'Neal, Pat, GEN—78, 103, 110

Oneichuk, Sergei, CPT [ah-nyey-CHOOK], [seer-GYAY]—155, 165, 174

Panzarella, Roy, LTC—155

Patton, Neal, COL—7, 10

Pern, Stephen—143

Petnicki, Vlad, CPT [PET-neet-skee]—79, 88, 126

Perry, William—24, 71, 104

Podkolzin, Yevgeny Nikolaevich, COL GEN [paht-KOHL-zeen], [yiv-GYEH-nee] [nee-kah-LAI-yih-veech]—43, 46, 107

Popov, ..., GEN [pah-POHF]—43

Prokudin, ..., COL [prah-KOO-deen]—175

Protosevich, Robert, CPT [pruh-tah-SYEH-veech]—177, 179, 181

Pushkin, Aleksandr Sergeyevich—159

Radzinsky, Eduard [rahd-ZEEN-skee]—107

Reimer, Dennis, GEN—93, 94

Richie, ..., Dr.—73

Rieff, David—77

Rodionov, Igor, GEN [ruh-dee-YOH-nuf], [EE-guhr]—111, 160

Ryabov, Aleksandr Ivanovich [RYAH-buf]—94, 95

Rybkin, ..., GEN [RIP-keen]—108, 111

Savin, Aleksandr Pavlovich, Major [SAH-veen], [ah-leek-SAHNDR] [PAH-vluh-veech]—167

Scanameo, Andrew, Dr. (Major) —73, 74

Shalikashvili, John, GEN—24, 154, 155

Shamilin, Yevgeny Georgievich, COL [shah-MEE-leen], [yiv-GYEH-nee] [gee-OHR-gyeh-veech]—64, 65, 97, 112, 144

Shevtsov, Leontii Pavlovich, COL GEN [shif-TSOHF], [lee-OHN-tee] [PAHV-luh-veech]—31, 32, 33, 36, 37, 39, 76, 77, 82, 97, 98, 99, 107, 111, 113, 125, 159, 175, 176

Zhirinovsky, Vladimir [zhih-rih-NOHF-skee], [vlah-DEE-meer]—31, 86
Zubak, Kresimir—177
Zyuganov, Gennadii [zyoo-GAH-nuf], [gyeh-NAH-dee]—14, 99

Printed in Great Britain
by Amazon

41775130R00117